Gardening on Pavement, Tables, and Hard Surfaces

Gardening on Pavement, Tables, and Hard Surfaces

George Schenk

TIMBER PRESS

Published in 2006 by
Timber Press, Inc.
The Haseltine Building
133 S.W. Second Avenue, Suite 450
Portland, Oregon 97204-3527, U.S.A.
www.timberpress.com
For contact information regarding editorial, marketing, sales, and
distribution in the United Kingdom, see www.timberpress.co.uk.

Designed by Karen Schober.

Printed through Colorcraft Ltd., Hong Kong

Library of Congress Cataloging-in-Publication Data

Schenk, George.
Gardening on pavement, tables, and hard surfaces/George Schenk.
     p.   cm.
ISBN-13: 0-88192-812-9 (paperback)
ISBN-10: 0-88192-812-7
1. Gardening   I. Title

SB453.S34 2004
635.9'67–dc21   2003048406

A catalog record for this book is also available from the British Library.

Dedicated to the gardener who dares

Contents

PREFACE

This book introduces adventures in garden artistry and entertainment that are mostly unknown: the making of gardens on pavements, on tables, and on other plantable platforms such as rock tops, railings, stumps, and logs. I began in 1964 by constructing and planting a small "island" garden on a paved terrace (Plate 33), which was followed in 1978 by a much larger garden consisting of beds of plants on the paved parking area of a friend's property, a place that begged for plantings where there was no open ground for them. Those first pavement beds of mine are still growing vigorously (Plate 21). Their location is in New Zealand, one of several countries where I garden each year on pavement and all sorts of platforms, as well as in open ground. Most of the gardens are on the properties of friends whom I visit yearly, devoting a month or two or three to each friendship and to each garden. Such is my life and gardening career since I retired from my mail-order nursery business, The Wild Garden.

I'd be finished if it weren't for my friends. They welcome me when I arrive and display no noticeable relief when I eventually leave. Ours is an extraordinary sort of symbiosis: I the migratory gardener, they the providers of refuges in need of gardening. And this fellowship has worked for us these many years. (In just a moment I'm going to explain what all this may have to do with you and your gardening.)

My widely disbursed gardens and garden friends are situated in the cool tropical mountains of northern Luzon, Philippines; in the tropical lowland of Samar Island, also in the Philippines; in the Mediterranean-like climate of Auckland, New Zealand; and in the temperate climate of coastal British Columbia in Canada and of the Pacific Northwest in the United States, where I began gardening in 1948 on family property near Seattle. The great variety of plants I grow in these locations and their broad range of acclimation add up to a gardening experience applicable to many places, including, I will hope, your garden. Then, too, the methods of gardening I write about are workable anywhere in the gardening world.

This book is in part a manual on what to plant and how to plant it on platforms. It is also an account of some memorable occasions in which friends and I have been brought together by one of humanity's more effective social agents, ornamental plant life. Come join in the good times. Several of them are on the exotic side.

WITH GRATITUDE

Wherever you read somebody's name in these pages, please know that I've placed it there with a sense of gratitude. These are people who have helped in making the gardens or in providing information about the gardens and plants described in this book. Or, they have provided photographs as a gift. And oh how grateful I am to all the garden jobbers, though unnamed, who have helped with the construction and care of gardens that I blithely write of as mine.

A good garden friend that I've named several times in these pages, Mo Yee of Auckland, deserves being named again, with gratitude, for having typed up the book from my fifty-thousand words of longhand, making the manuscript accessible to my Timber Press editor Linda J. Willms. It has been uncommonly rewarding to work with this professional. On dozens of pages Linda has made suggestions for sharpening the manuscript, suggestions I've followed gratefully. Never once has she attempted to schoolmarm me into silence by balking at my several neologisms in the book (horrors to any conservative technician in English) or at several probably outrageous zingers of mine.

CHAPTER ONE

The Babylonian Connection

Platform gardens of all kinds and sizes—
from the bed of plants on pavement at
ground level, to the tabletop landscape, to
the stroll garden on the paved roof of a
high-rise—are alike in being supported on
hard surfaces that are usually impervious to
roots and to water. They share that charac-
teristic and one other: Platform gardens are
generally quite a surprise. They tingle the
mind of the viewer with the electricity of
amazement, while provoking the mind with
a piquant and intriguing sense of illogic:
What is that garden doing *there*?

PLATE 1: Babylon revived:
a modern-day hanging garden.

The enigma of the platform garden is ancient in gardening; its present-day representations have an illustrious antecedent in the Hanging Gardens of Babylon, circa 605 B.C., envisioned by Nebuchadnezzar or by some creative dreamer among his palace advisors. Greek historians of the sixth century A.D. describe the garden as being 3 or 4 acres (1.2 or 1.6 hectares) in extent and supported on a series of progressively stepped-back brick terraces, which also served as the roofs of palatially appointed rooms. The uppermost terrace held the main garden at a height of about 100 feet (30.5 m) and was multiply waterproofed, first with a thick covering of asphalt strengthened with dry reeds, and on top of that layers of mortared tiles or bricks, and finally sheets of lead. Over all, a deep spread of soil sustained a variety of large trees kept green with water hoisted mechanically to the terraces from the river Euphrates. The visual effect of the Hanging Gardens was said to be that of a verdant mountain. The psychological effect, in a desert setting of eye-puckering glare and mineral barrenness, must have been that of arrival in paradise.

Great architecture on a huge scale such as this requires a great client; that is, one willing to let the vision proceed to reality unimpeded, and able to spend bags of money. Apparently, no other hanging gardens were ever afforded for many centuries following the demise of the Babylonian Empire, for there are no records or even legends of any. Yet at least three major hanging gardens of relatively recent making remain with us as examples of the art time-honored enough to be considered historic. The earliest of these is a grove of massive oaks atop a centuries-old tower in Italy. The next

in time is the early twentieth century's—and today's—Bridge of Flowers in the United States. More recent is a roof garden in England, where, in addition to a lavish display of smaller plants, hardy palms rooted in a 3-foot (90-cm) depth of soil stand as jauntily as telephone poles with pom-pom canopies.

Now we live, as we have since the late twentieth century, in what may well turn out to be the all-time heyday of hanging gardens, several of them approaching Babylonian size and opulence. Many architects of our era, rejecting the austere International Style of the mid-twentieth century and reverencing the new Green Religion, have garnished their buildings with lawns, flower beds, shrub borders, trees, festooning vines, even plantings of prairie wildflowers and grasses. Nearly every big city in the Western world now has its examples of architecture externally planted—and often in the interior as well.

I've heard expressions of discomfort from a few people who want their gardens on the ground and their buildings in the clear, but for others among us, the greening of architecture helps satisfy our need to live and work close to plants, to have them there as part of our daily lives. We may expect an increasing call for high-rise landscaping as wilderness diminishes and as home gardens become available to fewer people.

Babylonian Revival. Much in the manner of the original Hanging Gardens is the stepped-back series of planted terraces in Plate 1. These lead (out of sight) to a roof garden of mowed lawn and a vine-covered pergola. On the lowermost terrace are beds of impatiens, a hemlock tree (*Tsuga*), and Loderi rhododendron hybrids; at mid-level are maples (*Acer circinatum* and *A. palmatum*) and ferns (*Polystichum*); at top, maples with *Pieris japonica*.

PLATE 2. Prairie planting on a rooftop.

Rooftop Prairie. Plate 2 shows prairie grasses and flowers growing in a timber-framed, 28-by-19-foot (8.5-by-5.8-m) bed of soil originally 2 feet (60 cm) deep, now settled to about 16 inches (40 cm). On purpose, the garden is unwatered, unfertilized, and (so far) unweeded. The garden architects hope that this shaggy bed of wild vegetation will serve as a miniature habitat for butterflies and other worthy insects, and even for nesting birds. (Any especially airy soil mix of, say, compost and sand won't sustain prairie plants in a bed that is not irrigated. These plants are designed by Nature to inhabit loamy soils, which retain a slight but crucial moistness during drought.)

The idea of an ecological benefit in roof gardening has inspired several plantings of rough grass and small wild perennials on America's Pacific Northwest rooftops, in soil only 3–4 inches (7.5–10 cm) deep. Nonetheless, this soil depth is sufficient to soak up, with the assistance of the plants, an annual tens of thousands of gallons of rain water and so reduce poisonous flooding through storm sewers into salmon streams. If you are thinking of placing such an environmentally kindly coat of soil and plants on your home roof, remember that engineers advise strengthening the roof first. Even a 3- or 4-inch depth of soil requires a roof six times stronger than one covered with shingles.

Maple on High. For a couple of decades I've walked along a sidewalk below a rooftop Japanese maple (*Acer palmatum*) and have looked up at it with a sense of refreshment. Always a great sighting, the tree is shown in Plate 3 at the start of its autumn leaf coloring, which goes on into a fiery red. Recently I bluffed my way onto the roof and found that the tree measures about 24 feet (7.3 m) wide by about 17 feet (5.1 m) high, without ever having been pruned other than to remove a few shade-weakened lower limbs. It grows with other plants in a bed 75 feet (23 m) long by 6½ feet (2 m) wide, in soil that was 2 feet (60 cm) deep when supplied but has settled to much less. Irrigation is by sprinkler

PLATE 3. High-rise maple.

heads; fertilizing has been infrequent but apparently adequate. The roots of the maple have by now interwoven to such chain mail density that not even weeds grow beneath the tree, but top-dressing with new soil would make the space inhabitable.

Bridge of Flowers. America's premier hanging garden grows on a bridge in Shelburne Falls, Massachusetts, and is known as the Bridge of Flowers (Plates 4 and 5). The town proudly proclaims the garden as the only one of its kind in the world. More than that, it is one of the world's more effectively spellbinding works of landscape gardening.

The bridge itself dates from 1908 and was built across the Deerfield River to extend trolley service to a neighboring town located a mile (1.6 km) or so beyond the far bank of the stream. Twenty years later the trolley run was discontinued, the bridge left to pedestrians and to upstart weeds. A thriving growth of weeds on an abandoned, raised structure such as this bridge is always a wondrous example of the will of plants to take hold and inherit. It also can be powerfully suggestive to garden-minded people. (At the present time, for instance, a faction of New York City citizens is campaigning to save a disused, lushly weedy and even bushy, elevated train line just as it is—an impromptu garden.)

The idea for the Shelburne Falls bridge garden first took hold in the minds of a local couple, Mr. and Mrs. Walter Burnham, who then goaded the townspeople into a gardening mode. From the start, the construction and maintenance of the garden have depended on volunteer labor, donated and bequeathed money. The first work of actual gardening came when soil was placed on the

PLATE 4. The Bridge of Flowers in Shelburne Falls, Massachusetts. Five hundred kinds of plants thrive in this 400-foot- (122-m-) long disused bridge. Photo by Don Normark.

bridge, to a height of 30 inches (75 cm) along its railings and a depth of 9 feet (2.7 m) in its hollow support columns. The latter have an ancient precedent in the structure of the Hanging Gardens of Babylon, whose soil-filled support columns provided deep root-runs for trees, as do the loamy columns of the Bridge of Flowers more than two and a half millennia later.

Today, in its bountiful depths of soil, the bridge supports some five hundred kinds of flowers, shrubs, vines, and trees. Those who stroll along the bridge's medial pathway are presented with a visual banquet and may partake of it as a metronomic viewer, walking down the middle of the bridge and incessantly glancing left and right at the parallel border plantings, or as a linear viewer, concentrating on the border at one side during the outward trip, the other side during the return. It is, of course, a choice far too strict for the more stimulated visitor, who rather tends to buzz back and forth to flowers on one side and the other as randomly as a bumblebee.

PLATE 5. Plants root in a lavish 30-inch (75-cm) depth of soil on the Bridge of Flowers. The perennial at center is the sea holly *Eryngium amethystinum*. Photo by Don Normark.

CHAPTER TWO

Pavement Gardening

Pavement gardening is the transformation of inert pavement into lively garden. The changeover is accomplished in various ways:

■ By covering pavement with soil, framing the resulting raised bed with some material solid enough to hold it in place, and then landscaping the bed

■ By planting low ground covers (pavement covers in this situation) in the seams of soil between the paving blocks of a terrace or a patio

■ By planting low growers closely about a walkway of paving stones or concrete pavers, so that pavement and plants form a garden unit

PLATE 6. A pot of *Coleus* placed at the edge of a shaded pavement bed for the summer brightens an evergreen display of the fern *Blechnum capense* and of the flowering plants *Bergenia*, *Cymbidium*, and *Astelia*.

▪ By planting grass or ground covers in the open grids of preformed concrete gridwork used in covering the soil of a driveway or a parking lot

▪ By allowing shrubbery or ground covers that grow in soil beside solid pavement to grow over it to some extent—pavement gardening by glorious overflow, as some of us see it

Each of these methods will be detailed in turn in chapters two, three, and four, beginning with gardening in a bed of soil on pavement.

The Making of Pavement Garden Beds

The reasons for converting a paved area into a garden bed are sound. Soundest of all, and applicable to many properties, is accident prevention in places where aging pavement has settled or buckled and exposed a treacherous edge that would almost certainly trip someone eventually. Placing a garden on the bad patch will not only neutralize the danger but also may transform dangerous and unsightly pavement into landscaping that will rate as one of the property's most attractive features. The cost and commotion of such a transformation will be considerably less than sledgehammering or jackhammering the offending pavement into movable pieces, hauling it away, and then perhaps replacing it with a new spread of the same material. Of course, the greening of pavement can only be done at a place where pedestrians may easily skirt the garden bed.

Another good reason for creating a bed of plants on pavement is that it offers a better alternative to conventional container gardening. Plants are often more generous in growth and in flower production in the roomier root run of a bed of soil on pavement than in pots or tubs. The planted bed is also more presentable than many a patio or walkway container garden clutter of planted boxes, crockery, and plastic.

Pot gardening may, however, be combined with pavement gardening to the benefit of both, by placing pot plants (ideally in containers of a uniform style or of similar appearance) closely in front of the planted bed, as in Plate 6, where the plants within the bed and those in front will enhance each other's display. Alternatively, plants in pots may be added to the planting within the bed. Potted plants of tall and lanky form, awkward on their own, are among the best for fitting into beds of pavements plants; here the spindleshanks borrow basal foliage from their leafier neighbors, which often hides their pots as well as decking out their gaunt stems. Admittedly, this gardening by subterfuge may violate the sensibilities of the purist landscaper, but the ploy has as a mentor no less a gardener than Gertrude Jekyll, pasha of the perennial border, who dropped pots of flowering lilies into her border plantings for summer color, cunningly fluffing the surrounding leafage about the terra-cotta to conceal it.

Yet another motive for pavement bedding is to gain ground for plants on a home lot that has been paved to death, as often happens in contemporary property development, clear paving (as in the clear cutting of timber) being less costly and bothersome to the developer than designing and setting aside small areas for gardening. Paved areas hardly big enough for people and the family chariot(s), let alone plants? I refuse to believe it. A courageous gardener can always find an expendable patch of pavement here and there that may be comman-deered and converted into a garden bed or bedlet. In addition, even if your pavement landscaping is a triumph of art over practicality, the latter loses too few arguments with the former and clearly deserves to lose this one.

The Shape of the Bed. Should the pavement garden bed be free form or straight along its sides ("curvilinear" or "rectilinear" in the argot of land-scape architects)? The answer depends, as a rule, on the setting: If the setting is predominantly of straight lines in walls or terracing or plantings, or in the pavement itself, then straight lines in the bed will usually more appropriately harmonize this addition with the existing garden. Conversely, a free-form bed will usually fit best in a free-form garden setting, but not always. A bed formally geo-metrical in shape—oblong or T-shaped, square or round—may provide welcome relief from the leafy shag of a garden otherwise informal, and vice versa. You can visually test the suitability of a formally or informally shaped bed by outlining the proposed bed with garden hose, string, or sticks, changing the shape until it suits your sense of artistry and accom-modates any undeniable demands of pedestrian or vehicular traffic.

Suitable Plants. As the nursery industry has demonstrated in recent decades, virtually any kind of ornamental plant in the world can be grown in a container of the right size, containing the right soil. In that gardening on pavement is a grander form of container gardening, it seems probable that any tree, shrub, perennial, or other plant of

terrestrial life habit can be grown in a pavement bed, as long as the climate, soil depth and compo-sition, and the available amount of sun or shade, water, and fertilizer are to the plant's liking. There is one additional proviso: When grown in pave-ment beds, some plants are slightly less hardy than those same kinds growing in open ground, so avoid planting species known to be touchy in your winter climate.

Kinds of Soil. The best soil for pavement garden-ing is friable (crumbly), airy, and fast draining owing to an abundant content of humus and sand or pumice. Such soil is suited to all types of pave-ment gardens and plants—trees, shrubs, garden perennials and annuals, succulents including cacti, epiphytes that will accept terrestrial life, ferns, and mosses. The least suitable soil would be heavy with clay, relatively airless, and slow to drain away water. In a friable soil, air spaces between the soil particles encourage the onward progress of roots through the ground, which in turn stimulates branch growth and leaf formation. An adequate supply of air in the soil promotes growth addition-ally by discharging excess water and by assisting the plant to absorb certain elements vital to it.

Nature's soil deluxe, known as loam, consists of humus (flecks of decaying vegetation), sand (bits of decaying stone), silt, and clay (stone particles much smaller than sand). From the latter two soil increments, plants absorb minerals essential to life. Loam by itself might be too dense in texture to be a wholesome medium for pavement gardening but, as an ingredient in a soil mix, provides plants with a constant natural supply of mineral food. Because of its relative expensiveness and weightiness, loam is left out of most commercial soil mixes. Some bedding "soils"—not to be recommended for pavement gardening or any other kind—leave out not only loam but sand as well and are made up merely of humus (often finely ground tree bark or rotted sawdust). The consequent total lack of most minerals essential to plant growth must be made up for by a carefully scheduled regimen of applying fertilizer to plants grown in the medium. In time, straight humus (as a commercial product though not necessarily in Nature) tends to settle and compact into a hard and airless mass, anathema to plant life.

Probably a hundred commercial soil mixtures will serve pavement gardening perfectly well. Minor variations in their ingredients are of no great consequence. One of the best commercial mixes I've used in pavement gardening contains equal measures of composted garden gleanings (pruned branches and pulled weeds obtained by the truckload from garden jobbers), sphagnum peat (not sphagnum moss but the substance that lies underneath, centuries older and far less airy), and builder's sand (whose particles average about barley-corn size), along with a liberal lacing of pumice, and a fertilizer containing trace elements plus nitrogen, phosphorus, and potash. The inclusion of pumice, rather than vermiculite, as a soil weight-reducer and aerator is to the good. As recent findings have revealed, some forms of vermiculite are like asbestos in being carcinogenic if dust from the mineral is inhaled. Moreover, when constantly moist in garden use, vermiculite breaks down within several years and becomes a gooey sludge.

Another soil mix I've used and found suitable contains sandy loam, garden gleanings, builder's sand, and sedge peat (rotted sedges and other swamp vegetation) in equal measure.

A third commercial blend, one I've not worked with but which is much used by landscape architects and contractors for roof gardens (certainly a type of pavement garden), is made up equally of garden gleanings, finely ground tree bark, and builder's sand. This recipe is more often chosen for its relatively low cost than for any superior value as a growing medium. Even so, it matches other, more expensive mixes in growing plants splendidly if kept adequately fertilized and watered.

If you will be blending a soil for a pavement garden, an ideal mix might contain two parts composted and screened vegetation (such as gardening gleanings, rotted sawdust, sphagnum moss, peat, rotted hulls of grain, or coffee grounds), one part builder's sand, and one part loam (an ideal but optional ingredient). Blend all ingredients thoroughly with a shovel, at a time when they are dry enough to pour, rather than fall in clods, from the side of the shovel blade.

Other optional ingredients for the mix include up to a half part of pumice or rotted animal manure; or a scattering of poultry manure, ground charcoal, or water-absorbent, water-doling polymer crystals; or as much as one full part of used mushroom compost, a mildly stimulating, long-lasting plant food made of steamed and essentially sterile horse manure or, more often nowadays, chicken droppings (mind those black crumbs of compost that adhere to button mushrooms brought home from the market). Any of these soil amendments will better the soil mix. All of them are extras of a nicety, but none is vital to perfect success in pavement gardening.

The Right Depth of Soil for the Plants. In making a pavement garden bed, the right depth of soil depends on the kinds of plants you would grow and on how big you would have them grow. With exceptions, the larger the potential growth of the plant, the deeper the soil needs to be to allow the plant to approach that potential, but if you want the plant to stay small, or at least to grow slowly toward large size, give it a shallow bed. (The ultimate dwarfing and slowing effect of scanty soil is apparent in the art of bonsai.)

Taking into account the cost of the soil, if you will be buying it, and of the material needed to retain the soil bed at its sides, the less you need of either, the better for the budget. It helps that plants are highly adaptable to soil on pavement that is shallower than the soil in the wild places they inhabit or even the open ground of the garden. A soil bed as shallow as 4 inches (10 cm) will grow healthy carexes, luzulas, and other grass-like plants of small habit and, with only minor dwarfing effect, certain sizable perennials, among them *Agapanthus, Astelia, Pilea microphylla, Rhoeo,* and the bromeliads *Neoregelia, Nidularium, Vriesea,* and *Aechmea.* It will also grow a host of frost-tender succulent plants, notably *Agave saponaria* and *A. vera,* echeverias, crassulas, and haworthias; hardy ground-covering ferns such as *Adiantum venustum* and *Polypodium;* many mat-forming plants such as the hardy, small-leaved ivies; the tenderish *Heterocentron (Heeria), Laurentia,* and *Polygonum vaccini-*

ifolium; fully hardy *Sedum album, S. reflexum,* and *S. sediforme;* carpeting thymes; and *Campanula poscharskyana* and *C. portenschlagiana.* (Poscharsky and Portenschlag will likely be resented to the end of time for their jawbreaker names applied commemoratively to those two campanulas.)

I've grown all these plants in soil no more than 4 inches (10 cm) deep when laid down. A little probing of their beds with a spade a couple of years later has revealed that the soil has shrunk to a depth of about 2½ inches (6.5 cm)—still deep enough for the healthy growth and happy flowering of plants already well established *before* the soil shrank. Those same plants might or might not have grown if they had been *planted* in soil of that scanty depth.

A soil depth of at least 6 inches (15 cm) is enough to produce vigorous growth and madcap flowering in all sorts of annuals, rock garden and alpine plants, perennials, and shrubs of up to 2 feet (60 cm) or so. It also supports middling ferns, though of course these have no flowers.

A 9-inch (23 cm) depth of soil will foster a bountiful harvest of cucumbers and leaf lettuce along with other leafy vegetables and herbs. It will also provide a reasonable crop of tomatoes, corn, potatoes, and other root vegetables, although the latter would really prefer a foot (30 cm) depth of soil, as would rhubarb, a deeply rooted plant.

A pavement bed at least 16 inches (40 cm) deep will support most kinds of small trees—those that usually attain 15 to 20 feet (4.6 to 6.1 m) at maturity— including fruit trees, but will tend to reduce their growth. Among small growers often chosen for pavement gardening, especially for roof gardens, are staghorn sumac (*Rhus typhina*),

Japanese maple (*Acer palmatum*), and other small-ish maple species. While the sumac tolerates drying winds, the Japanese maple is intolerant of the winds that afflict many roof gardens, yet is otherwise certainly one of the most accommodating minor trees for pavement gardening in the world's temperate latitudes.

Trees of larger size, such as oaks (*Quercus*), ginkgo, sweet gum (*Liquidambar*), the taller kinds of magnolias, and many others, are also grown successfully in pavement gardens. It seems a safe guess that most kinds of shade trees will grow perfectly well on pavement, but their height will probably be considerably less than it would be if they were growing in unlimited soil. Landscape architects often provide roof garden trees with lavish beds of soil 2 feet (60 cm) deep, even 3 feet (90 cm) deep in the case of an aforementioned roof garden in England; however, those 2-foot-deep beds tend to settle to 16 inches (40 cm) or so and are never, in my observations, topped up with new soil or mulch (a restorative step usually not specified, as it should be, in landscape plans and in job descriptions for contracting gardeners). An annual surface scattering of soil or mulch would serve as a tonic not only to the trees but also to underplantings of shrubbery, perennials, or annuals.

A soil bed 16 inches (40 cm) deep is also adequate for the planting of privacy screens formed by columnar evergreen trees, among them various clones of American arborvitae (*Thuja occidentalis*), or by such tall grasses as sugar cane (*Saccharum officinarum*), the major forms of Eulalia grass (*Miscanthus sinensis*), and clump-forming bamboos (*Bambusa ventricosa* is especially useful in pavement gardening). The great grasses, once they anchor themselves with their substantial roots, are usually not troubled by windstorms, but a columnar evergreen or a shade tree growing in a pavement bed might be especially vulnerable to wind of gale force. To minimize any danger, prune such trees to a low height that still provides shade or screening.

How Much Soil Will You Need? Figuring the cubic yards of soil needed to make a pavement garden bed of a given size and shape requires only simple arithmetic, but the equations vary somewhat depending on the shape of the bed.

To determine soil needs for a square or oblong bed, first measure the length and the width of the bed-to-be and multiply these two measurements to obtain the square footage of the area to be gardened. Now multiply the square footage by the depth of the soil to be placed, which for the purposes of our illustration is 1 foot. The result is the number of cubic feet of soil needed to create the bed. Divide that number by 27, the number of cubic feet in a cubic yard, and the quotient will show in cubic yards the amount of soil needed to cover the area.

Here is a sample equation for finding the cubic yards of soil needed to place a 1-foot-deep planting bed on an oblong, 16-by-8-foot area of pavement:

$$Length \times Width \times Depth = Cubic\ feet$$
$$16\ feet \times 8\ feet \times 1\ foot = 128\ cubic\ feet$$

then

$$Cubic\ feet \div 27 = Cubic\ yards$$
$$128 \div 27 = 4.75\ cubic\ yards$$

Four and three-fourths cubic yards of soil will be needed for the bed, but soil suppliers usually don't sell by the quarter or half yard, so you would need to order at least 5 yards for this particular job. You might want to order a yard or two more than that, for reasons I will expound in a moment. For now, more arithmetic.

To determine the amount of soil needed for an L-shaped bed, simply divide the bed into two rectangular beds, calculate the cubic yards for each bed using the above formula, and add the two subtotals to find the total number of cubic yards needed.

To determine the quantity of soil needed for a free-form or circular planting bed, take three pairs of measurements of the bed's varying length and width. Multiply each of the three lengths and widths separately to obtain three calculations of square feet. Add up those three square footages and multiply by 1 foot, the depth of the bed, to obtain the number of cubic feet. Divide that sum by 83. The figure you obtain will represent—roughly—the cubic yards of soil needed for the bed. (If the bed is highly irregular, take four or five sets of length and width measurements and add them separately; divide the sum of four sets of measurements by 109; five sets, by 135.)

For shallower or deeper soil in a pavement bed of any shape, extrapolate from the amount needed for a 1-foot (30-cm) depth. For a 6-inch (15-cm) depth you will need, of course, only half as much soil as for 1 foot; for an 18-inch (46-cm) depth, half again as much.

Gardeners working with metric measurements will need to first multiply length by width by depth (in meters) to obtain cubic meters, and then multiply the number of cubic meters by 1000 to find the number of liters. The formula for a rectangular bed is as follows:

Length x *Width* x *Depth* = *Cubic meters*
5 meters x 3 meters x 0.3 meters = 4.5 cubic meters
then
Cubic meters x *1000* = *Liters*
4.5 x 1000 = 4500 liters

As I was saying awhile back, you might want to buy somewhat more than the amount of soil your calculations indicate—for several reasons. First of all, for use as topping soil. Soil mixes usually arrive in an aerated and expanded condition (beneficial to plants) from the actions of the mixing machinery along with the admixture of any kind of porous humus. Within a year or two after the soil is placed in the new bed, it will naturally settle and compact by as much as one-third. You can take charge of soil settling by walking, but not stomping, all over the new bed immediately after placing the soil. Your footwork will effect at once much of the settling that would otherwise occur over time, allowing you to top-up the bed right away with extra soil. An additional topping of soil or mulch will be needed in the long term.

Then, too, it is handy to have extra soil, stockpiled or bagged up and stored in some hideaway spot, ready for use in any conventional container gardening you may do (pavement gardening being container gardening of dashing unconventionality), even if it is nothing more than filling a few pots with soil and surplus plants from your burgeoning garden, perhaps with the idea of giving the surplus away.

Speaking of gardening in the giving vein, the sudden manifestation of a partial or full truckload of soil at the front of your property in public view may provide opportunities to brush up your nice-neighbor image. There it stands, in steaming glory, Mount Fertility, a seemingly inexhaustible resource, surely enough and more than enough for your garden and others. Some worthy neighbor, and even one's own spouse for that matter, will likely look at that magnificent pile, decide that you can spare some of it, and ask for a bucket or two for his or her own projects. This has happened to me more than once when I've had soil delivered, and I won't be at all surprised if it happens to you. To grant the needy one that bucket or two, or even a couple of wheelbarrow loads, is no more than an exercise of horticultural noblesse oblige.

All that I've said so far about measuring soil for the pavement bed pertains to soil purchased by the yard. Buying soil by the bag is more expensive than buying it in bulk and hence less casually given away. You will need roughly 20 big gunny-sack-size bags full to equal 1 cubic yard (1250 liters), but if you are better at arithmetic than I, measure the three dimensions of a single soil-filled bag and figure fairly exactly from that one bag the number of bags you will need in total.

Placing Soil in the Bed. A raised bed of soil on pavement whose sides are steeper than 45 degrees will require retaining of some sort, and even a bed with gently sloping sides will be safer for being retained in any garden where pets or small children with digging instincts have access to all that inviting earth. Whether the soil is shaped into a bed

first, then surrounded by retaining material, or the retaining installed first, then the inner space filled with soil, depends on the choice of retaining material (see below). In either case, the soil at the time you work with it should be moist but not overly wet. A waterlogged soil is unduly heavy and unwieldy, with a tendency to cake, which makes soil shaping difficult. If possible, schedule the job of pavement garden construction in rainless weather, but if hard rain is imminent, protect a delivered load of soil with tarpaulin.

If the soil is to be placed before the retaining material, convey the soil to the job site and dump it on the pavement in the rough form of the bed to be. If you don't have a garden cart or a wheelbarrow for the haul, you might use a tarpaulin or even an old tablecloth for a two-person carry. Once the soil is in place, shape the bed with a shovel, then trod over it lightly to help settle it, as has been suggested previously and I now repeat for emphasis. After your footwork, add soil to raise the bed to the height you want it to be and refine its shape with a rake.

The procedure is identical for placing soil after retaining material has been installed, except that the bed will have already been shaped by the retaining and will only need to be walked on to settle the soil, and then topped off to raise the soil to the proper height.

In Plate 7, the 7-inch- (18-cm-) high beds have been shaped and compacted with a shovel, a rake, and shod feet. The vertical sides and the

---

PLATE 7. In the foreground, a pavement bed newly shaped on top of dangerous up-edged concrete. Beyond, pavement beds with plantings of sweet woodruff (*Galium odoratum*).

straight perimeters of all the beds have been suggested by the formal lines of the terrace itself. The bed in the foreground is now ready for a retaining material or a planting for retainment.

A Choice of Retaining Materials. A considerable array of materials may be used as retaining for pavement garden beds, some of which are, as a rule, installed more conveniently before placing the soil that makes up the bed, others more conveniently afterward. Prior-to-soil retaining materials include railroad ties, timbers, planks, and bricks; post-soil materials include driftwood, interlocking concrete blocks designed to hold back soil, and certain ground-covering, soil-retaining plants that I will name. Stones or riprap (slabs of broken concrete paving) may be placed as unmortared retaining either before or after placing the soil, depending on their stability when stacked. Rounded stones probably should be placed only after the soil, but angular stones or riprap are usually stable enough to be stacked into free-standing walls up to a foot and a half (45 cm) high. With these latter two materials you have the choice of walls before soil or afterward.

Retaining with Railroad Ties. When used to retain soil, railroad ties (or sleepers as they are known in Britain and Australasia) are of a greatly variable life span, depending largely on how deeply the creosote used to preserve the ties has penetrated the wood. The deeper, the better, but deeper also means the more lastingly nasty the treated wood is to hands and nose and clothing. Deeply creosoted ties remain perfectly sound 40 years

after installation in my Seattle-area garden—and had had trains running over them for 40 years or so before I got them—but steps I made for our garden in Auckland, New Zealand, out of nearly new but superficially creosoted sleepers are half-rotten 22 years later.

A single course of ties of a standard 7- or 8-inch (18- or 20-cm) thickness will retain that many inches of soil, a depth sufficient for the healthy growth of a great range of annuals, perennials, and small shrubs. I find that a single course of ties is weighty enough to stay in place, resisting the push of the soil in the raised bed, without being fastened together. Two or more courses of ties will require fastening. Use spikes, rods, or sawed off sections of steel pipe to hold them together. First drill holes into the wood of slightly smaller diameter than that of the spikes, rods, or pipe, and then drive the metal home with a sledgehammer.

The corners of railroad tie retaining may be right-angled, formed simply by placing the butt end of one tie against the side of another, or the corners may be acutely angled by sawing the ends of the ties to shape. Let me dissuade you from using a handsaw for the job, as I once did. Sheer folly. Railroad ties are tough customers and your sawyer's muscles won't recover for days (voice of experience). A chain saw is the proper tool for this job.

Retaining with Timbers and Planks. Six-by-six-inch (15-cm) timbers are a usual size for retaining soil. They are placed and fastened in the same way as railroad ties. Timbers that have been pressure-treated with wood preservative may last as long as

30 years in garden use; timbers that have been sur-face-treated with preservative, as long as about 20 years; untreated timbers, usually years less than two decades.

Planks measuring 2 by 10 inches (5 by 25 cm) and pressure-treated with preservative are espe-cially serviceable for retaining a raised bed. You might use narrower or wider boards, but boards thinner than 2 inches (5 cm) are not recom-mended because of their relatively short life when in contact with soil. One method of fitting planks together into a frame for soil retainment is to nail the planks to 3-by-4-inch (7.5-by-10-cm) stakes placed in the inner corners of the frame. Elbow iron fasteners (shaped like door hinges, but unbending) offer another means of holding the frame together sturdily at its corners.

A newly constructed wooden frame is apt to appear, in the words of an archaic American saying, as homely as a mud fence, but the plain frame may be covered over and dressed up splendidly with cascading shrubs or perennials planted in the soil along the upper edge of the frame. The plant covering need not be total, and in fact the framed bed is usually more interesting as a garden feature when some of its wood is left in view. Frame-cov-ering plants will descend from the top at a rate of about 5 to 10 inches (13 to 25 cm) yearly, and will be improved by pruning away any branches that stick outward fairly straight rather than cascade. Some of the plants I've used as foliar falls and found to be first-rate for the purpose are *Coprosma arenaria, Cotoneaster congestus, Dryas octopetala, Hed-era helix* 'Needlepoint', *Helichrysum argyrophyllum* 'Mo's Gold', *Heterocentron, Juniperus horizontalis,*

Microbiota decussata, Pilea microphylla, Polygonum vacciniifolium, Rosa 'Flower Carpet', and *Rosmari-nus officinalis* 'Prostratus'. Most of these are described in a list to come.

Retaining with Driftwood. Driftwood as a land-scape element imparts a rustic quality suited to a rural garden, especially one with a shoreline. The sides of a pavement bed that is to be retained with driftwood should be sloped at about a 40- to 70-degree angle. After shoveling and patting the soil (with the back of the shovel blade) to make a neat slope, compromise it by scooping shallow trenches in the soil in which to slightly nestle each piece of driftwood, leaving much of the wood exposed. For maximum stability, the pieces of wood should be about as big as dolphins and dalmatians. Let wood rest on wood so that the pieces are mutually sup-portive. Don't be concerned about the gaps that remain from place to place between the irregular driftwood pieces. The soil will stay in place, and you can make excellent use of these gaps by planting them with rock garden–size shrublets or perennials, thereby converting a bank of sculpturesque drift-wood forms into the arboreal equal of a rockery—a woodery, if you will.

Driftwood may be long- or short-lived in garden use, depending much on the species of tree from which the wood came. The driftwood of resinous conifers often remains sound for decades when in contact with garden soil, but that of many other kinds of trees often decays too rapidly—from soundness to punkiness within a few years—to be a sensible choice as retaining material. Even so, I've sometimes used short-lived driftwood for small jobs of soil retaining, knowing the wood's predisposition full well, but acting on a gardener's sensibility beyond sensibility, the joyous dash of doing a thing, getting it done, and enjoying it, even if only for the short term.

Retaining with Stones, Bricks, or Concrete Riprap. All my considerable experience in using stones as pavement garden retaining, and the one job in which we used bricks, has been in climates with warm or relatively mild winters, where temperatures at their lowest rarely reach 0°F (-18°C). Here, the stones and bricks have always stayed in place through the winter, never any problem. In subzero regions, however, brick or stone retaining will be subject to the pushing, dislodging actions of deep freezing. There, a wall of bricks set up to hold a bank of soil might be wrecked by frost action. Stone retaining will be more frost-resistant than brickwork, especially if the stones are sizable, unmortared, and placed firmly in contact with each other on a sloping bank of soil. Vertical retaining with large stones, 200 pounders (100 kilogramers) or bigger, should be winter-safe well below 0°F (-18°C). I've never used concrete riprap to retain soil but would suppose it to be safer still than large stones if big pieces were set flat atop one another like a stack of soda crackers. I'm partly guessing at all this and suggest that, if you live where winters are severe and are considering the use of stones, bricks, or riprap as retaining, you ask a local engineer or landscape contractor what can or cannot be done.

We used bricks—my brother Ken and I did— to retain a raised bed of soil on concrete in his Seattle-area garden where winters are moderate. The bricks were old and mellow, having been made in 1905, we knew, Ken having salvaged them during a remodeling of his house, built in that year. We stacked them only four bricks— about one foot (30 cm) high—without mortar, and found that they stayed in place, just barely, when we filled in behind them with soil, after which the bricks needed a little tamping back into line. Clearly, if we'd gone higher with the bricks to support a deeper bed of soil, we would had to have used mortar.

The first year we planted the brick-sided bed with Yukon Gold potatoes purchased from a mail-order nursery whose catalog listed nearly one hundred potato varieties and pointed out Yukon Gold as being the best seller (Plate 8). We placed these starter spuds at about 16-inch (40-cm) intervals *on top of the soil* in the bed and mulched them deeply with straw to induce the formation of new potatoes directly, or nearly, on the surface of the soil.

Now, no crop may be more illogical for a backyard gardener with a pavement bed than a crop of potatoes. After all, potatoes are available year-round at prices well below the cost of growing them in a garden structure. Yet, no adventure in home gardening is more magical than the unveiling of potatoes when the crop is ready. Up from the earth or out from a mulch, they bring on the same thrill, no doubt, as that of recovering

---

PLATE 8. Potato plants in a pavement bed retained with unmortared bricks. Tubers form directly on a soil surface deeply mulched with straw. Harvesting requires no digging, merely the removal of the mulch.

buried doubloons. The digging of onions or beets doesn't quite match up. Our crop of Yukon Gold was not copious—fewer than a hundred tubers, but those few were delicious and remain in mind as an accomplishment I count on savoring for a lifetime. Everyone who gardens should grow potatoes at least once (also corn and tomatoes).

In years afterward Ken's wife, Phyllis, has taken over the brick bed and grown ample quantities of leaf lettuces, cucumbers, crookneck squash, and herbs.

Retaining with Plantable Concrete Blocks.

Bare concrete blocks, newly placed to retain soil, amount to a decidedly ungardeny feature, one more in keeping with an alley in an industrial part of town. Nevertheless, when planted with vegetation that has the potential to grow over and mask the concrete, and that greenery having been given ample soil, water, fertilizer, and time to grow— where did those unsightly blocks go? As you see in Plate 9, they have largely disappeared beneath leaves. These blocks had been placed on pavement at the edge of a driveway to hold a yard- (0.9-m-) high bank of fill dirt. By the end of the second summer after planting, as shown in the picture taken 3 October, the minor portion of the blocks left in view is not at all unsightly and is even interesting as garden architecture.

These precast blocks are one of a number of styles on the market designed to support steep soil while providing plantable interspaces. In this

PLATE 9. A retaining wall of gardenable concrete blocks well furnished with plants.

style, the 12-inch- (30-cm-) tall, 20-inch- (50-cm-) wide blocks with their 4-inch (10-cm) thickness of concrete are weighty enough to hold back a tonnage of soil and generous enough, with their 12-inch-wide soil pockets to give plants root space in which to revel. The partying community of perennials and low shrubs in view includes *Carex comans* 'Frosted Curls' (synonym *C. albula*) at bottom, in silvery grass-like leaf; *Geranium sanguineum* at bottom, with magenta flowers; an aureate form of *Phormium tenax* at top; an African daisy hybrid (*Osteospermum barberiae*) with scattered flowers; *Sedum spectabile* at center, with its attractive seed platters; a sprawling hybrid rose at upper left, labeled *Rosa* 'Flower Carpet'; *Nepeta* 'Six Hills Giant', the gray-green foliage at center; at right one of the compact Oregon-Pacific Michaelmas daisy hybrids, in form a mound of green with a million flower buds ready to pop; and barely in sight at the left-hand margin of the plate, a few gray branches of French lavender (*Lavandula dentata*). In all, a range of foliages from large to small, from slender to broad, in a well thought-out complement of sizes and shapes, and a variety of plants that present something or another in flower spring, summer, and fall.

An equally effective planting to cover the harshness of newly placed concrete blocks can be achieved by setting out one kind of plant on the entire wall. The effect will indeed be equal to, but quite different from, that of planting an entertaining variety of foliages and flowers. With one kind of plant over all, you forfeit the entertainment in favor of a sense of substantiality and of serenity that comes with uniform foliage; and if the plant is a flowering kind, the sweeping uniformity of bloom offers the viewer a certain perplexity, a soothing excitement.

Any of the larger plants of retaining value, in a descriptive list to come, will make handsome covering over concrete blocks. But how little I know. Note that the plants in Plate 9, only one of which appears in my list, have all worked out rather well as concrete coverers, as would a thousand others you might choose. You might ignore my recommendations totally, go plant shopping as an explorer of the unknown, and still come out right. This is exactly the way I've always shopped for plants I know nothing about, to be known in growing them.

Retaining with Plants as Plugs or as Upholstery. Many kinds of plants will lend themselves to the job of retaining the earthen sides of a raised pavement garden bed. Some fifty of the best sorts for the task are named in the forthcoming list I keep referring to, a listing that might quite possibly be expanded to five hundred. The criteria that make most plants usable as soil retainers include a compact habit, dense branching and foliage, and substantial, soil-clutching roots. A few plants that I've found useful in retaining soil actually lack the roots for it (*Neoregelia* is one such), but compensate by having foliage full enough to keep water from eroding the soil.

The plants employed in covering the sides of a raised bed usually differ from the kinds planted on the top of the bed. I say *usually* because it occurs to me that a person could set out the same plant over all, bed sides and top as well. I myself

have not yet done so but can visualize the plain and bold appeal of it. After deciding on the kind or kinds of plant with which to green-wall the bed, choose whether to upholster the sides with mats of greenery or whether to plant a platoon of plugs. The term *plug*, in garden parlance, is a homely old horticultural coin which has not been recognized and given place as such in any of several dictionaries I've consulted. The garden plug is a small plant division or sod that is plugged, usually as one of many plugs, into the ground at intervals with spaces of open soil in between. Some of the ground covers useful in pavement gardening which are especially willing to be divided up and planted as plugs include *Galium, Laurentia, Ophiopogon, Sedum album, S. reflexum,* and *S. sediforme, Thymus,* and *Zoysia*; all these are described in the famous list to come.

Plate 10 shows plugs of a ground cover in place on the vertical sides of a pavement bed; the plugs as shown have grown considerably since I planted them and are now well on their way to uniting but are still recognizable as separate plant divisions. The ground cover variety is *Saxifraga moschata* 'Alba', a "mossy saxifrage," a plant not quite tough enough to merit being added to my list of best kinds for retaining. I had loaded up a cart with it at a garden center, purchasing the plant simply because it was the most economical thing they had that I could use—economical in that the plants could be divided at once. The 4-inch (10-cm) pot plants on offer overflowed their containers well down over the sides, quite as exuberantly as a glass of beer with a wild head. At home I took a knife to these mossy saxes and divided each into three rooted pieces—plugs in this instance—which I inserted at 8-inch (20-cm) intervals in the sides of the pavement bed. It is easier to plant plugs of ground covers on a slope rather than on vertical soil, as I have done.

Very small plugs of certain ground covers will take hold on a soil slope and spread into a solid cover if you can take extra-good care of them as they grow. Sedums may be the most economical and rewarding of ground covers to plant out as small pieces. Buy one generously full 4-inch (10-cm)

PLATE 10. A pavement bed (the newly shaped bed of Plate 7) planted at the sides by the plug method using *Saxifraga moschata* 'Alba'.

pot plant of a spreading *Sedum*, divide it into, say, twenty-five branches with or without a bit of root on each branch, plant them at 4-inch (10-cm) intervals in fertile soil of fine tilth, keep them weeded and watered (gently, to prevent soil erosion), and maybe keep them covered with netting to dissuade soil-scratching birds, and you may see those sprigs of *Sedum* grow into twenty-five matlets of ground cover by summer's end, each of them the diameter of the original plant.

PLATE 11. Retaining the sides of a pavement bed by the upholstery method using sweet woodruff (*Galium odoratum*).

The alternative style of planting the sides of a pavement bed uses a ground cover as upholstery, covering the soil all over, at once, with portions of some mat-forming perennial. Buying enough flats filled with a ground cover suited to the job would be a sizable expense. I can only hope that you, as I, are able to avoid such high cost by having grown a quantity of a suitable ground cover ahead of time and now have it available for harvesting. In my own situation I have available, in the open ground of a couple of the properties where I garden, broad colonies of such ground covers as creeping thyme (*Thymus praecox*), *Galium*, *Waldsteinia*, and *Sedum album*. These I had set out years earlier as single small pot plants and they have grown generously. I harvest them for pavement gardening by scooping them up from the ground in pancake- or pizza-size portions with a spade.

In Plate 11 I am installing a harvested mat of sweet woodruff (*Galium odoratum*) as upholstery on the side of a pavement bed on our Seattle-area terrace. The plant had been taken up from the open ground with soil on its roots, a factor that reduces shock during transplanting. Now the mat's under-part of roots and earth is being firmly pressed against the raised bed's wall of compost. The next step will be to sift loose compost from a shovel or trowel blade to cover the exposed top edge of the ground-cover mat and to fill any air pockets that remain between the plant's root mass and the side of the bed (an exploratory plunge with a trowel will reveal pockets in need of filling). Plate 7 shows pavement beds (in the background) retained at their sides with upholstery plantings of sweet woodruff.

The Maintaining of Pavement Garden Beds

Pavement garden beds, like gardens in general, require care to keep up appearances. Watering, weeding, fertilizing, and pruning are as much needed here as elsewhere.

Watering. A new planting, whether on the top or the sides of a pavement garden bed, requires thorough watering immediately after its installation and constant moistness of soil during its first summer. By the end of that time most plants will have extended their roots well into the soil bed; after which, depending on the thirstiness of the kind of plant, water needs may differ greatly.

An established pavement garden is as bibulous as the thirstiest members of its plant community or as abstemious as the drylanders in the composition. It would not be altogether practical to combine such guzzlers as astilbes and gentians with such camels as cacti and other succulents. But, it is possible to do so if you will be watering by hand: Simply direct the water toward plants that need it and away from those that don't want it. The esthetics of combining drinkers with drylanders are another matter. The differing natural habitats of the plants have given them dramatically disparate forms and coloration which only a garden artist (you, I trust) might combine successfully.

Water all kinds of pavement garden plants exclusive of xerophytes every several days in cool cloudy weather from spring through fall, when no rain falls to take care of the job. Water every day in hot, dry weather from spring through fall. Water enough in winter to keep the soil moist.

While plants with average needs for moisture (most of the plant kingdom) will with gratitude drink up a daily application of water during dry weather, they may be capable of surviving 2 days without water during drought if you and the rest of the household are away for that time and if no friend is available for the task. Plants in a shaded bed, it may be encouraging to know, are more able to withstand dryness (up to several days of it) than those in a sunny bed. However, I had better add as a disclaimer that even 1 day in dry soil is risky to many plants growing in shade or sun.

An established pavement garden planting of succulents usually requires irrigation only after a month or so of drought, but if you want to keep succulents growing during dry weather, keep them watered. In a desert climate (surprisingly to me) even some of the most xerophytic succulents— small cacti of many sorts—when grown in gardens will not prosper unless watered during prolonged dry weather.

Weeding, Pruning, Dead-heading, Thinning, and Shearing. Weed, prune, dead-head, thin, and shear the pavement garden as needed to keep it from deteriorating, as would surely happen to this or any garden if uncared for. The relatively low maintenance garden is a possibility depending on choices of plants, but any *no*-maintenance garden is all too soon a jungle or an Ozymandian desert of lifeless plant remnants.

Fertilizing. The following suggestions for fertilizing pavement garden beds apply as well to all other types of pavement gardens and other platform gardens. First among basic facts about fertilizing is that the continuing vigor of virtually all kinds of plants—trees, shrubs, vines, perennials, annuals, and edibles—grown in a bed on pavement or on other platforms depends on their being provided with a supply of the vital minerals in a suitable fertilizer. Possible exceptions include certain lichens which may be damaged by being doused with fertilizer, and many bromeliads, which may never need fertilizing. Specialists are undecided about fertilizing bromeliads, but I, for one grower, am a believer in the effectiveness of feeding neoregelias, vrieseas, tillandsias, and others right along with the rest of the garden.

Some commercial soil mixes that you might use in making a pavement garden bed contain fertilizer whose benefits will probably last for at least several months after planting the bed; the supplier should be able to tell you approximately how long. If, however, you have bought a soil mix that contains no fertilizer, or have put together a homemade mix, an addition of fertilizer is usually needed to round out the menu of essential minerals in the mix.

Slow-release (also called controlled-release) fertilizer is an excellent choice for use in pavement gardening and other platform gardening, on all manner of plants. The product comes as a boxful or bagful of pearly little beads. The initial application may be mixed into the soil or scattered on its surface. Over time rain water and irrigation will slowly release minerals from the beads, making them available to the plants. This constant fertilizing lasts about 4 to 8 months, depending on the strength of the product (the package label usually gives an expected time limit). When the food value of the beads is finally used up, scatter a new supply over the surface of the bed and right up to the basal stems of the grateful plants. Slow-release fertilizer is notably easy and safe to use: I've never heard of overdosing being a problem with these beads.

Dry fertilizers in the form of grainy and slightly dusty chemical compounds are entirely usable but with precautions. Read the package label to determine the recommended dosage for a given amount of ground—usually about a quarter cup (70 ml) of fertilizer for each 4 square feet (0.4 sq m) of soil surface (4 square feet is approximately equal to the spread of two pages of a broadsheet newspaper). Take care not to use too much; an overdose will render the soil toxic to plants for a year or more. Avoid inhaling any dust that flies when you work with the fertilizer. Wear rubber gloves to protect your hands from chemical burn. In making a new bed, scatter the fertilizer over unplanted soil and then turn it into the ground with a shovel or garden fork. A sufficient application in springtime will usually keep plants fed through an entire growing season. Repeat the application the following year and in years thereafter by scattering the fertilizer over the soil, in between any permanent plants in the bed, and then hosing it into the ground immediately. Wash away any dust particles or grains of the fertilizer that lodge on plants; if left on, the chemicals will kill leaves and even entire plants. The one overriding attraction of dry fertilizer is that it is considerably less expensive than other kinds.

PLATE 12. Squared-off pavement beds retained with unmortared stones. The planting includes New Guinea impatiens (in flower) and *Coleus* (in the background).

Acidifying fertilizer is a wettable type usually sold as food for rhododendrons, camellias, and other acid-loving plants. I find it to be much more than that and have used it (and no other fertilizer during some years) with splendid payback in growth and flowers on plants as varied as rhododendrons, roses, alpines, bonsai, bromeliads, shrubbery, ferns, grasses, orchids, annuals, and cacti growing in pots; in pavement, tabletop, and rock-top gardens; and in open ground. I have yet to meet a plant that does not thrive on acidifying fertilizer, not even that famous calciphile, edelweiss. An acidifying fertilizer has special value when used in pavement garden beds built on new concrete. During the concrete's first year after having been poured, and to a lesser extent for several years following, a caustically alkaline effluent will exude from the Portland cement in the pavement to the detriment of plants whose roots encounter it. An acidifying fertilizer neutralizes the effluent and nullifies its harmful effects.

Whatever kind of fertilizer you use must provide a total mineral diet for the plants and can only do so if it contains tiny amounts of certain so-called trace elements along with more substantial quantities of the basic three elements that foster plant growth and flowering. The basic three are nitrogen, phosphorus, and potassium, the latter listed as "potash" on most package labels. A product that contains all three of these elements is sometimes termed a complete fertilizer. The term is misleading. No fertilizer supplies complete nutrition to plants unless it contains traces of such elements as iron, manganese, zinc, copper, boron, and molybdenum. If there is no listing of such on the package, these ingredients are absent from the fertilizer, and your plants will pine for them unless, with rare good luck, they all happen to be naturally present in the soil you've used for the bed.

The percentages of nitrogen (N), phosphorus (P), and potassium (K) in a fertilizer are coded in three numbers on the package label: 8–10–4, for example, or 20–20–20, or 20–6–12, and so on with quite a lot of hokum and hucksterism involved. Fertilizers now come to market in a fantastic variety of codes. On a recent tour of the fertilizer shelves in a garden store I counted eighteen different N–P–K recipes for plants and plantings of such singularity as roses, "small fruits" (berries, that is), bulbs, flower gardens, vegetable gardens, tomatoes, trees, lawns, and even clematis, along with other plant categories. The shelves also held "rhododendron and camellia food," the acidifying fertilizer I spoke of earlier, which is compounded for use on the eponymous plants and all others of the hundreds of kinds of acid-seekers. It is a product of honest distinction. As for those other fertilizers in the N–P–K arsenal, they are usable interchangeably with about equal benefits to plants in general. One bag, box, or bottle will do for the whole garden. If you happen to have rose food or bulb food or whatever on hand, go ahead and use it, if you are of a mind, in fertilizing the pavement garden. There will be no problem and definite betterment when you apply fertilizer of any kind judiciously.

PLATE 13. Sweet woodruff (*Galium odoratum*) trimmed as a hedge after flowering. A spade has been used to clear the plant, roots and all, from the interior of the bed in preparation for a summer planting of *Impatiens*.

To Trim or Not to Trim. During springtime and summer, certain ground-covering plants used as siding on pavement garden beds will make growth that you may find excessive and may want to trim back neatly or even to hold in a formal line, that of a clipped hedge, at the sides of the bed. Ground covers planted on vertical pavement bed sides lend themselves more readily to formalization into little hedges than do plantings on sloped bed sides. In addition, the formality or the informality of the ground cover depends entirely on your own preference. For myself I have it both ways. I let the ground covers that I use as retaining for raised beds on pavement flower and fluff up at will during springtime (see Plate 16); after they flower, I use hedge loppers to trim back the outward growth of the plant and a spade to cut back the inroads the plant has made at the top of the bed (Plate 13). The pruning precedes the planting of impatiens in the bed for summer color. (The ferns, including *Polystichum munitum* in the foreground, are permanent here.)

The most billowy plant I've used as retaining is sweet woodruff (*Galium odoratum*). In midspring it converts itself into an earthbound cumulus of white, honey-and-horehound-scented flowers. After the flowers go (a few sprigs of which we will have picked in their prime and infused in stem glasses of Chablis or another dry white vintage, making the beverage into May wine of tradition, to be sipped in celebration of springtime and flowers), I rather enjoy the little chore of formalizing the plant for the summer, trimming it back into the lines of a boxwood hedgelet. The formalizing of the *Galium* requires, in addition to the post-floral

pruning in late spring, two additional touchups with the hedge loppers during the summer. Easy work—the plant is soft of tissue—and a satisfying little hobby in itself.

Others among pavement garden retaining plants that seem, to my eyes, better for being pruned once a year in late spring or early summer are any of the dwarf forms of *Hedera*, *Campanula poscharskyana*, *Waldsteinia*, and *Iberis*.

Step Up for Your Award. Once you've engineered and landscaped a bed of plants on pavement, and have it growing well, a time for congratulations is at hand. Let us hear, in mind at least, a silvery fanfare of trumpets in honor of your work of garden art and craft, unique in the world, and of your own creativity. The Greeks gave their heroes a crown of laurel; your own coronet is in the form of the foliages you've added to an area of broken or barren pavement. Walk proudly there. Walk entertained.

Soil-Holding and Frame-Covering Plants of Top Value

Here are fifty or so plant species and varieties selected from hundreds of ground covers that I've grown and tested over the years. Most of these selections have proved to be outstanding as small- to medium-scale erosion-preventers when planted on sloped or vertical soil beds and on banks up to about 4 feet (1.2 m) high. Others have special values (indicated in the write-ups I've given them) as edging in table gardens or as drapery, growing downward over the visually harsh sides of framed beds.

In assigning hardiness, I've used the United States Department of Agriculture's numerical rating system: the higher the number the less hardy the plant. The average annual minimum temperature ranges are as follows:

CELSIUS	ZONE	FAHRENHEIT
Below −46	Zone 1	Below −50
−46 to −40	Zone 2	−50 to −40
−40 to −35	Zone 3	−40 to −30
−35 to −29	Zone 4	−30 to −20
−29 to −23	Zone 5	−20 to −10
−23 to −18	Zone 6	−10 to 0
−18 to −12	Zone 7	0 to 10
−12 to −7	Zone 8	10 to 20
−7 to −1	Zone 9	20 to 30
−1 to 4	Zone 10	30 to 40
5 and Above	Zone 11	40 and Above

When applied to plants, numbers 1 to 4 indicate hardiness at well below 0°F (−18°C); 5 to 6, hardiness near 0°F (−18°C); above 6, half-hardiness on up to frost-tenderness. I had better own up, though, that these numbers as I've attached them to plants in this book—and as far as that goes, as they have been attached to plants in two good garden reference books I have here in front of me—are decidedly imprecise. The hardiness ratings I see in print are in many cases way off what I know of these plants from my own gardening. Local conditions—a garden location in sun, in shade, on a hill, in a woodland, beside a body of water, in a windy site—may sway the hardiness of some plants by as much as two digits (from a 5 to a 7, for example) in two garden separated by only a couple of miles of terrain. The fact that the plant is growing on pavement may also effect its hardiness, reducing it perhaps by one digit.

Please read hardiness ratings for what they are, generalizations of some use, but with your own garden microclimate and a winter more severe than usual settling the final score. Local garden centers may be of help if you ask about the hardiness of some plant; however, the most up-to-date and dynamic garden centers—those that constantly introduce plants new to their areas—may be the least sage in ascribing hardiness. They may not yet really know, may have yet to hear from customers with praises or complaints about the plants' capabilities. The most sensible plan would be to stick with plants long grown and well known in your region. But then who wants to be always a sensible old stick when so many beguiling new plants are offered every glorious spring? After all gardening at its best is in part gambling. And now at last the top-value plants.

Adiantum venustum. Evergreen maidenhair. Zone 5. A ground-covering fern from the Himalayas of India with aerially divided fronds, held about 12 to 16 inches (30 to 40 cm) high, spreading by stolons to about a yard (0.9 m) wide within several years. A gardener-friendly plant, never dying out if given half a chance, a fern with a liking for morning sun and afternoon shade or daylong filtered shade. The roots and stolons weave themselves into a mesh dense enough to hold soil on the slopes of a pavement bed; they give rise to foliage more buoyant than that of any other soil-retaining ground cover, in contrast to the many other useful ground covers that express sturdiness and stolidness. Propagate this fern from sods no smaller than a pork chop, cut from the parent plant early in autumn or very early in spring.

Calluna vulgaris '**Dainty Bess**'. Zone 4. One of several dozen named selections of Scotch heather, this one a gray-green mat about 5 inches (13 cm) high and 18 inches (46 cm) across in 5 years. A choice edging or retaining plant for a sunny pavement garden. Lavender bloom in late summer spikes at the tips of the branches. Pleasant flowers over superb foliage: soft to the eyes and touch, a seeming moss mound with a gray overlay on its leaves that suggests frostiness sufficiently to cool mind and body on a hot summer day. Several other low-growing selections of Scotch heather may also be employed as soil-holders on pavement garden slopes. To control their height, clip them back in early autumn or spring.

Campanula poscharskyana. Zone 1. A leafy green ground cover, 1 foot (30 cm) tall. A great splash of blue-violet star-flowers in early summer. Shade or sun. Drought-tolerant. Plant from divisions set out at intervals of 1 foot (30 cm) or less.

Coprosma arenaria '**Tepuna**', *C. arenaria* '**Hawera**', and *C. martinii* '**Tiako**'. Zone 7. These similar New Zealanders form dense masses of thyme-like leaves on string-slim branches. Their growth is essentially flat or low and mounding, to several feet across, conforming to surfaces of soil or stones, dropping almost straight down over the sides of wood-bordered pavement beds. Distinguished, in a quiet way.

Cotoneaster congestus. Zone 5. A Himalayan shrublet of neat growth at moderate speed: soil-conforming, stone-clutching, inching forth on stiffly woody branches dressed with small, rounded, dark evergreen leaves and, in season, small, round, rose-red berries. I don't remember the flowers, which would seem to indicate that they are hardly noticeable or that I am deplorably unobservant or quite possibly both. The species is available in several named varieties, differing in their degree of "congestus"-ness (denseness) of branch, flatness of growth, and smallness of leaf.

Cotoneaster congestus '**Cooperi**' is especially flat in habit, with an instinct—most accommodating in platform gardening—to grow downward at about 9 inches (23 cm) yearly. It becomes a leafy curtain descending in air from the edge of a table, or over sloped soil, or closely conforming to any pavement bed framing material.

Cuphea hyssopifolia. False heather. Zone 8. More like a pillowy, shrubby thyme than heather. Tiny, dark green, lance-form leaves. An abundance of tiny summer flowers, purple, magenta, mauve, or white in the several forms of the plant. Prefers sun, adaptable to half shade. A plant of especially easy disposition when set out as a soil holder on the sides of beds or flat on pavement. Let it sprawl or prune it to a formal line. Cuttings root easily.

Cytisus decumbens. Zone 5. A shrublet of Mediterranean origin. Whenever I learn of such nativity in any woody plant I immediately associate certain imperatives with the species—and they are operative in this one: a demand for sunshine, a tolerance of drought, a need for fast-draining soil, and a contentment with impoverished ground. This deeply rooting, soil-binding broom of flattened branch habit grows to 6 inches by 3 feet (15 by 90 cm) after several years, turning into a green hummock made up of hundreds of slim and flexible branches, blazed over with thousands of bright yellow pea flowers in springtime. On cloudy spring days I have gone out into the garden, caught the glow of this plant in the corner of my eye, and thought for a moment—here comes the sun.

Daboecia cantabrica. Irish bell heath. Zone 5. Native to moist peat moors but surprisingly tolerant of short-term dryness when established in a garden. Tiny, dark green leaves on upright branches clustered together to form a basket-like shrublet. Racemes of lantern-globe flowers, purple, white, or pink in various named forms, over a long summer season. Clip it back after it flowers to keep it compact, at a foot (30 cm) or less in height; unclipped, some forms of the *Daboecia* would grow lank of branch, to about 18 inches (46 cm) or higher.

Euonymus fortunei. Zone 3 or 4. This evergreen shrub native to Japan makes sprawling growth far and wide, rooting down as it goes, ramping over stones and even up walls. It is far too big and boisterous to be used as a soil support in the gentle art of pavement gardening, and most of the dozens of named forms of this species are likewise outsize for our gardening, but several horticultural varieties and one natural form of the species are perfectly suited. These will grow in shade or sun and are hardier than English ivy, which they replace in cold-winter climates where the ivy can't survive.

Euonymus fortunei '**Emerald Gaiety**' is a low, upright grower with close branches and small leaves, dark green with a bright white edge. It is superb as a miniature hedge-edging for pavement garden soil that rises about 1 to 2 feet (30 to 60 cm) high. Clip the shrublet to shape, as I've done with *Galium odoratum* in Plate 13, or let it grow naturally. I'm an admirer of a certain 'Emerald Gaiety' hedge which grows on flat ground beside a sidewalk that I frequent. The hedge, now nearly two decades old, is kept pruned to about 16 inches (40 cm) wide and high, and stays densely leafy year after year in all seasons. The natty green-and-white leafage gives the pedestrian a perk that is especially welcome on a gray winter day. 'Emerald Gaiety' is a choice (read, fairly slow-growing) shrublet to be set out one foot (30 cm) or less apart.

Euonymus fortunei '**Emerald 'n' Gold**' is another fine cheer in winter, with small yellow-edged leaves. Low-growing and moderately spreading, with a mainly upright and open branch pattern, this variety will provide sturdy cover for a pavement garden slope up to about 3 feet (90 cm) high.

Euonymus fortunei '**Kewensis**', a miniature variety, makes an eminently useful small-area ground cover for a pavement garden slope about 1 to 2 feet (30 to 60 cm) high. In habit it is a ground-hugging vinelet with intricately branching stems so slim as to seem like green spaghetti with leaves. The leaves are a mere ¼ to ½ inch (6 to 13 mm) long, light green with an intriguing pattern of pale veins. Set out small pot plants at about 10-inch (25-cm) intervals for full cover after one summer's growth.

Euonymus fortunei **var.** *radicans,* winter creeper, is a determined spreader, but not too big to use as a cover over concrete blocks, which it will make disappear beneath dark green elliptical leaves on trailing branches.

Fragaria chiloensis. Beach strawberry. Zone 4. A sand-and-soil-binding wild strawberry native to the Pacific coast of the Americas, growing as a low carpet of glossy evergreen, three-part leaves and white saucer flowers, in sun or part shade. Set out starts 9 inches (23 cm) apart in spring for full cover by fall. The white-flowered forms of beach strawberry almost never set fruit when growing in gardens.

Fragaria **'Panda'** is a hybrid of *F. chiloensis* with sassy pink flowers and a scattering of tasty little wild strawberries—never more than a few.

Galium odoratum (synonym *Asperula odorata*). Sweet woodruff. Zone 1. A mat of wheel-shaped leaves with leaflets as spokes. The foliage—evergreen in mild winters—is covered over in springtime with a froth of tiny white flowers. Unclipped, the plant makes billowy, foot- (30-cm-) tall growth; with pruning, it is a dense 6 inches (15 cm) in height. This fast-spreading ground cover may be divided into small, rooted clumps (plugs) in spring or fall and set out at about 8-inch (20-cm) intervals for full cover in one summer.

Gaultheria miqueliana. Zone 4. A Japanese alpine. The species is the most enduring of the low-growing rock garden gaultherias that are adaptable to pavement gardening. In sun about a foot (30 cm) tall, in shade even taller; a slow stroller to about 2 feet (60 cm) across in 7 or 8 years. Small, oval leaves, matte evergreen, with crackle-pattern veining. Tiny white flowers and long-lasting showy white berries with wintergreen flavor. Most birds dislike the fruits and leave them alone. A 49-year-old patch of this plant carries on in one of my gardens and will, I expect, cheerfully see me out.

Gaultheria procumbens. Wintergreen. Zone 3. Native to eastern North America, a 4-inch- (10-cm-) high mat-forming shrub that makes an especially neat ground cover on a low pavement-garden slope in part shade or filtered shade. Drought intolerant and, unluckily, beloved of root weevils. Expect to lose part of a planting in any garden region where these little monsters are prevalent. The leaves are small, egg-shaped, dark green, leathery, and lustrous. Small, white, bell-form flowers in the spring are mainly hidden by the leaves but are followed by bright red bead berries well in view and held for months. The plant is the original source of oil of wintergreen, the flavoring and scenting agent now largely replaced by one of those approximations brought to us through chemistry.

Hakonechloa macra **'Aureola'.** Zone 4. A subtly variegated grass (Plate 30, the yellow-leaved plant in the center) of a darker and lighter yellow-green. Native to Japan. Graceful, with arching grass blades in a clump, to about 18 inches (46 cm) tall, 30 inches (75 cm) across in 3 years. Stays put; does not romp or seed about. Another form of the species, **'Albo-aurea'**, makes a clump of flashy, white-variegated green blades. Plant either form in filtered shade or sun.

PLATE 14. An ivy-capped breezeway.

Hebe '**Carl Teschner**'. Zone 5. Patch-forming shrub, 1 foot (30 cm) tall, 3 feet (90 cm) wide in 5 or 6 years. Glossy green leaves, ¼ inch (6 mm) long, lance-form, dense on their branches. Springtime flowers, violet-purple and showy, produced on short spikes. Sun or half shade. Propagate by clipping off rooted branches and planting them where you want them to grow.

Hebe pinguifolia '**Pagei**'. Zone 4. One of the hardiest and most garden-reliable of the several hundred New Zealand *Hebe* species, clones, and hybrids in cultivation. A flattened shrub to 9 inches (23 cm) tall, 4 feet (1.2 m) across in about 6 years. Half-inch (13-mm) oblong leaves, chalky blue-gray with a rosy rim. Good show of early summer flowers, white in stubby spikes. Sun or half shade. Moderately drought tolerant. Branch cuttings taken in summer root readily.

Hedera helix. English ivy. Zone 4. The named forms of English ivy approach three hundred in number. Many are large-scale vines used as ground covers and wall covers. Many others, apparently small-leaved and short-stemmed when purchased as pot plants, explode in growth and leaf size when planted in open ground. A few remain circumspect enough of vine and reliably small enough of leaf to be given jobs as pavement garden slope-holders and as tabletop citizens (to be discussed in chapters seven and eight). Especially well suited, on those terms, are '**Needlepoint**', '**Green Feather**', and '**Ivalace**'. The first-named of the three, a plant widely available at garden centers, makes mounding, shrubby growth about 16 inches (40 cm) high and 4 feet (1.2 m) long, descending when planted on steep ground or at a table edge. Shade or sun. Drought-tolerant. For propagation in open soil, take branch cuttings back into old wood, in midsummer.

Helichrysum argyrophyllum '**Mo's Gold**'. Zone 9 or 8. South African. A small pot plant of this perennial, set on top of a pavement bed or atop vertical stonework, will drop straight down as a plait of silvery leaves and sunny yellow strawflowers. It will grow 6 feet (1.8 m) long in as many years if it has that much space in which to drop, but usually grows less than a foot (30 cm) wide. Planted on a slope, the growth fans out to a couple of feet (60 cm) across and perhaps three or four (90 to 12 cm) in length. A neat, flat grower with no need for pruning except perhaps to stop it at its downhill end. Full sun and fast-draining soil are best for this plant. When established, it may survive months of drought, although it will stop growing for the duration. The early autumn flowers stay bright for years in a dry bouquet, or last until you get bored with their dusty hanging about.

Heterocentron elegans (also known generically as *Heeria* and *Schizocentron*). Spanish shawl. Zone 8 or higher. A perennial of widely spreading, densely flat growth when grown in sun (Plate 32); somewhat open and upwardly striving in shade. A mid-green mat richly dressed with ½-inch- (13-mm-) long leaves (pointed ovals). During several weeks in summer the leaf mat is mostly covered by a dazzling display of hot rosy magenta flowers twice the size of the leaves. The plant will hold soil or cover frames and large stones—making them totally disappear, which you may or may not want to happen. Keep it away from other low-growing plants, which it will overwhelm. It is safe as a companion for tall perennials and for shrubs. Drought tolerant when established.

Iberis sempervirens. Evergreen candytuft. Zone 1. In time, a 2- to 3-foot- (60- to 90-cm-) wide mound of dark green needle leaves snowed over in springtime with clustered white flowers. Available in several named forms: '**Purity**', '**Snowflake**', and '**Snow Mantle**' are outstanding as low-growing garden-furnishing plants, as soil holders, and as showy flowers. '**Little Gem**' is often shy flowering but useful as a shrublet which may be kept clipped as a 4- to 5-inch- (10- to 13-cm-) tall hedge.

Juniperus horizontalis. Zone 2. Any of the numerous flat-growing, blue-gray named forms of this conifer will make serviceable shoring in pavement garden beds and curtaining plants at table garden edges. **'Bar Harbor'**, collected on the coast of Maine, is one such selection and is widely available. All the selection crave sunshine but will accept part shade.

Laurentia fluviatilis (synonym *Isotoma fluviatilis*). Blue star creeper. Zone 6. Dense, flat green mat of tiny leaves swarmed over by tiny azure stars in spring. Useful as a retaining plant or between pavers, where it will withstand considerable foot traffic. This species should perhaps be grown by itself, since it is invasive of any other low plants it meets as it spreads.

Lithospermum diffusum (synonym *Lithodora diffusa*) **'Heavenly Blue'**. Zone 5. A shrub whose branches sprawl radially from a central mound about 8 inches (20 cm) high. Leaves dark green, small, and narrow; little spring flowers of trumpet form, blazingly bright blue and abundant. At its best in full sun. Propagation is not easy for us amateurs, but have a go: take summer cuttings and root them under glass.

Microbiota decussata. Zone 1. A conifer from Siberian mountains, wonderfully distinctive for its trailing branches, soft and plumey in appearance, green in summer, turning bronzy in winter sun. Grows several feet tall and several yards across in open ground, but in pavement or table gardening limits itself to about 1 foot (30 cm) by 1 yard (90 cm) and attains that size slowly. Cascading growth when planted at the edge of a table. Sun, half shade, or all-day filtered shade.

Nandina domestica **'Harbour Dwarf'**. Zone 5. A dwarf form of the so-called heavenly bamboo of China and Japan. Grows 12 to 15 inches (30 to 37 cm) tall, slowly widening into a ground-covering clump of upright, toughly woody stems. The somewhat bamboo-like blade leaves are dark green with a bronze tinge in sun. Tolerant of shade. I've always found 'Harbour Dwarf' for sale as sizeable plants, about 10 inches (25 cm) across their spread of branches and leaves. Set out at approximately 20-inch (50-cm) intervals, these will grow to form a solid cover within several years. Propagate from cuttings rooted in a greenhouse or cold frame, or with daring and no certainty, from rooted stems cut at the periphery of an established plant and planted directly in the open garden.

Nandina domestica **'Pygmaea'**. Zone 8. Close, upright stem growth to more or less 18 inches (46 cm) high (Plate 96, the shrublet at the back). The green leaves turn to a flaming orange-red in hot sun and dryish soil. Useful as a ground cover when planted closely but eye-catching when planted as a specimen shrublet, together with low ground covers, on a pavement-garden slope. The plant is a popular old-timer in Mediterranean-type climates, but I've never seen 'Pygmaea' in a zone 5 garden center, where other named forms of *Nandina* are million-unit mainstays of the nursery industry.

Neoregelia. Zone 10. Tropical, withstanding only a light, brief touch of frost. These bromeliads, with their pineapple-top leaf tufts, reduplicating into clumps, make bold landscape statements (Plate 44, the plant at the lower left) and first-rate soil-holders on sloping ground. They are equally valuable when planted on pavements, on stones, and on tables, where they will make bushels of leafage on as little as an inch (2.5 cm) of soil. Certain of the *Neoregelia* species and many of the hybrids offer foliage that reddens attractively in sun, but the neoregelias must not be placed in daylong hot sunshine, which would scorch them. Give them morning sun and afternoon shade, or light, filtered shade.

Ophiopogon japonicus. Mondo grass. Zone 5. Japanese, as you will have got from the species name. A grass-like perennial, actually of the lily family, with bunches of purple flowers rather resembling grape hyacinths held up as little floral torches; flowers not produced in every garden. Curved, dark green blade leaves about a foot (30 cm) high in the typical plant, half that in the form **'Nana'**, which is just the right size for use in retaining small pavement garden beds. May be planted from divisions pulled (not very easily) from a clump of the plant and set out 4 to 6 inches (10 to 15 cm) apart. The divisions will grow slowly into clumps, the clumps into a solid cover. After a couple of years in place, a patch of Mondo grass will carry a noticeable accumulation of old, tired leaves. Clipped back, the plant will slowly regrow with fresh new blades.

Paxistima canbyi and ***P. myrsinites***. Zone 3 or 4. Respectively, a neat 10- to 12-inch- (25- to 30-cm-) tall shrublet from the mountains of Virginia, and a low, sprangly shrub from the Cascade Mountain foothills of British Columbia on down to California. The latter is easily pruned to shapeliness and

maintained at a height of about 18 inches (46 cm). Both paxistimas have slender branches dressed with little dark green, lanceolate leaves. The flowers are tiny and hardly noticeable. Demure in both leaf and bloom these species are nonetheless quietly appealing, a relief to those of us finally made nervous by horticulture's carnival of plants with loud leaves and flagrant flowers. Sun or part shade. Propagate by cuttings rooted in a greenhouse or coldframe.

Pilea microphylla. Zone 10. A frost-tender shrublet of tropical South American origin. Height and width about 16 by 36 inches (40 by 90 cm). Forms a low, broad mound in 3 years from a small pot plant, or from a mere rooted branch detached from an established parent and planted in shade or sun. The mounded growth is made up of an intricate mass of branches that are aerially spaced, succulent but slim, clothed in a lacework of tiny, kelly green leaves. In all, the plant vaguely suggests a merger of *Selaginella*, parsley (*Petroselinum*), and maidenhair fern (*Adiantum*). Prune it back if it outgrows its allotted space; regrowth comes surely and fairly fast. Tolerant of dryness. In some books, this plant is said to be short-lived or annual, but I know it in the tropics as soundly perennial.

Polygonum vacciniifolium. Zone 7. Vine-like growth, flat on the ground, branching about freely, conforming to rocks or pavement-garden frames, cloaking them with attractive, patterned leaves that turn red in hot sun and drought of which the plant is greatly tolerant. Tiny pink flowers, crowded on spikes in late summer. Invasive of any other low plants in its path, so best combined with tough shrubbery 1 foot (30 cm) or more tall.

Rhoeo spathacea. Moses-in-the-boat. Zone 9. Tropical but withstands a touch of frost. An 8-inch- (20-inch-) tall ground cover in its minor leaf form, nearly twice that height in the major form, widening at a rate of about 1 foot (30 cm) yearly. The plant grows as a colony of leaves in tufts, dark green above, purple underneath, some of both leaf sides showing. Also available in variegated leaf form. Small white flowers half-hidden in the leafage. Makes healthy, happy growth in soil as shallow as an inch (2.5 cm) deep or on fertile rocks in what would seem no soil at all.

Rosa. Zone 3. Ground-covering roses, such as the hybrids in the patented Flower Carpet series (available in red, pink, and white), produce pleasantly small flowers during the summer months on branches that will sprawl over and largely conceal a bank of plantable concrete blocks. These roses require pruning and weeding, the latter a troublesome task because of the need to plunge one's hands (gloved, of course) in among the thorny branches. The plants are probably too spreading in growth for use in any small-scale job of pavement garden landscaping.

Rosmarinus officinalis **'Lockwood de Forest'** and *R. officinalis* **'Prostratus'**. Zone 7. These are similar forms of the herb rosemary, both of them mainly flat in growth. Their stiff, somewhat brittle branches are densely dressed with little dark ever-green needles and are twice dense in springtime with small violet flowers that open closely over the foliage, pale violet in the form 'Prostratus', more richly colored in 'Lockwood de Forest'. Both are shrubs with all the sterling values for pavement gardening offered by *Cotoneaster congestus*: flatness and moderateness of growth, to a yard (0.9 m) or more across at about a foot (30 cm) a year), and a downward curtaining propensity. Both rosemaries are prone to the occasional loss of a branch due to breakage or blight.

Rubus calycinoides. Zone 5. Taiwanese in origin, a thornless raspberry, flat-growing at first, spreading widely, building up in time to a foot (30 cm) or even two (60 cm) in height, while making conforming growth over the rocks, blocks, or wood of pavement garden retaining (Plate 50, the plant in the foreground). Set out along the top edge of any of these materials the *Rubus* will grow downward a yard (0.9 m) or more, covering anything you don't want to see. The pavement garden bed probably should have nothing else in it that is smaller than a tree, for the *Rubus*, which grows simultaneously over ground and underground on stolons just below the soil surface, is tigerishly ready to overwhelm and suffocate any low-growing plant it comes upon. If, however, you with your pruning shears and with a garden knife for lopping back stolons are readier than the *Rubus*, then it will behave as a reasonably tame vegetative tiger. Valuable for its distinctive evergreen foliage, trilobed and rounded, olive green on the upper side with a deeply channeled surface, beige-colored and felty underneath. *Rubus calycinoides* produces little white cup flowers that show rose family membership. Most forms of the plant in the nursery trade set fruit sparingly, yet at least one form produces tasty, salmon-colored berries in plenty. So far, no selection of the species is being sold as a good fruit bearer; however, the hustling horticulture of the day, ever more sophisticated at an accelerating rate, may soon discover, name, and mass market just such a selection.

Sedum album. Zone 2. The typical plant, the only form really useful in pavement gardening, grows as a rapidly spreading carpet of beady evergreen leaves (Plate 33, the small-leaved plant at the bottom) and showy white flowers in midspring. Can be divided into mere fragments and planted about 4 to 9 inches (10 to 23 cm) apart, the closer, the quicker the cover. Especially useful as edging in pavement gardens. Grows well in soil as shallow as 2 inches (5 cm).

Sedum reflexum and *S. sediforme.* Zone 2. Two very similar species, often sold interchangeably, if identified at all. Both are dressed with gray-green needle-form leaves that are succulent and harmless to touch, and have yellow flowers in summer. In shade, these mat-forming plants take on a moss-like softness of appearance. They make firmer, denser growth in sun. These sedums form tough, drought-tolerant mats when grown in shallow soil on pavement or on stones. A clump of either species may be pulled apart into single branches; planted a few inches apart these will spread with satisfying alacrity.

Thymus. Thyme. Zone 5 without snow cover, zone 2 where covered by snow throughout winter. The

four carpeters and the single shrublet listed here rank among pavement gardening's most serviceable slope-holders and edging plants. All are densely clothed with little leaves about the size of capers or coffee beans. Best in full sun.

Thymus × citriodorus 'Aureus'. Lemon thyme. A twiggy, chartreuse-colored shrublet. Lavender flowers, a Fauvistic clash against the yellow-green foliage. To 1 foot (30 cm) tall or half that if kept clipped. Can be made into a miniature formal hedge.

Thymus herba-barona. Herb baron. A dark green, lavender-flowered mat, about 5 inches (13 cm) high, widening to 15 inches (37 cm) in a single summer, in good soil with good care (Plate 50). The lateral growth is typical as well of the other three carpeting thymes in this list. Some chefs rate this the best thyme for culinary use.

Thymus 'Pink Chintz'. A hearty green mat, lavender-flowered in early summer.

Thymus pseudolanuginosus (synonym *T. lanuginosus*). Woolly thyme. Two different plants are sold under this name. The best (now becoming scarce) is a vigorously spreading, flat, frosty gray carpet without flowers (Plate 55). Second best is a hybrid with a slight greenishness in its gray foliage. It is less vigorous in growth, with a sparse sprinkling of pinkish-lavender flowers.

Thymus "serpyllum" 'Wild Garden Form'. Makes a dark green mat with an especially full display of lavender flowers.

Vaccinium vitis-idaea. Lingonberry. Zone 4. Stoloniferous shrublet, 10 inches (25 cm) tall, spreading slowly to about 18 inches (46 cm) across in 5 years. Upright stems, ¼-inch (6-mm) leaves, in form shiny green ovals. Little bell flowers in spring, pale pink, in pendant racemes. Edible fall fruit like small cranberries. Half shade or sun. Intolerant of dry soil. Prey to root weevils in garden areas where this insect is prevalent. (Be courageous. Plant, but expect to lose 10 to 15 percent of the planting.) Harvesters of lingonberries in Scandinavia, where the species covers miles of moorland, add sugar to the raw berries and let them steep for at least several days. Then they are ready to eat, as a cousin of cranberry sauce.

Waldsteinia fragarioides. Zone 2. Leathery three-lobed leaves in a 3-inch- (7.5-cm-) high mat, green in summer, bronzing in winter sun. Small yellow saucer flowers in spring. An invaluable ground cover for sun or part shade. The strolling branches will drop down over, and cover, wood or mineral retaining a foot (30 cm) or more in height.

Zoysia tenuifolia. Korean velvet grass. Zone 8. Leaf blades dark green and fine in texture. May be planted inexpensively from small rooted pieces teased from a clump. Pleasantly meadowy in character if left untrimmed, but if you prefer to keep it short, trim it frequently. If left to grow tall and then cut back, this grass tends to die out.

CHAPTER THREE

Pavement Garden Tours

We've looked at the mechanics of converting broken or barren pavement into a lively garden bed, and I've pointed out half-a-hundred plants that are suitable for pavement gardens. Here now are real-life examples of pavement gardens.

Unsafe Pavement Made Safe with Planting

The hillside terrace in our Seattle-area garden dates from 1950 and its concrete paving has settled and tilted along its outer edge due to subsidence of the fill dirt on which the concrete was laid. It is a story commonplace in suburban land development: Fill dirt is dumped on a natural hillside and then leveled and compacted, according to building regulations, by running a bulldozer back and forth over it. In the long run, that is not enough. On our terrace, year by year, at a yearly rate of a small fraction of an inch, gravity has further settled the fill dirt, especially along its deeper, outermost side. By the 1990s the pavement at that side had settled unevenly and tipped upward, placing raised edges treacherously in the way of the unwary. I shall

PLATE 15. A pavement bed 3 years after planting.

PLATE 17. Newly set out plants of white *Impatiens*.

it is planted at the sides with plugs of *Saxifraga moschata* 'Alba'. The finished bed, shown in Plate 15 in its third year of growth, has a topside planting in place. The plant community includes lady fern (*Athyrium filix-femina*), feverfew (*Chrysanthemum parthenium*) in white flower, and *Hosta sieboldiana*, with grayish-green heart-shaped leaves.

The sides of another pavement bed on the terrace, upholstered with mats of sweet woodruff (*Galium odoratum*) in Plate 11 of the previous chapter, are seen again in Plate 16 with the sweet

PLATE 18. *Impatiens walleriana* and *Felix domestica* glorying in the shade of high summer. The pavement bed at bottom right, retained with *Waldsteinia ternata*, has been cleared for a late planting of carnations and *Nicotiana*.

always reproach myself for having not got around to neutralizing the danger by pavement gardening here in time, not until after the day my mother, in her mid-nineties, tripped on an upraised pavement edge and fell, sustaining bruises and a sprained shoulder but nothing worse, thank heaven.

And so I pavement garden here belatedly. Plate 7, in the previous chapter, shows beds of soil covering the tilted areas of the concrete terrace. The bed in the foregound is shown again in Plate 10 where

PLATE 16. A pavement bed with a planting of sweet woodruff in full flower.

woodruff in spring flower. In midspring the bed is lined out with plants of *Impatiens walleriana* (Plate 17), which later are in full summer glory (Plate 18). The bed at lower right of Plate 18, with a soil-supportive edging of trimmed *Waldsteinia ternata*, awaits a late planting in its topside soil. Later in the season, the sweet woodruff intergrows with the bed's winter planting of white pansies, soon to be retired (Plate 19).

The Parking Pad Garden

To Auckland now, where we garden on a steep hillside lot whose biggest and best piece of level ground, about 50 by 50 feet (15.3 m), had been paved for parking. In the 1970s, early days in my gardening here, I realized that the concrete parking pad was potentially the most livable outdoor part of the property. It seemed that the expanse of pavement was too good to lavish on vehicles alone, and I began converting edgewise portions of the parking pad into garden beds and landscaped space for living. The driveable part of the area now measures about two-thirds the size of the original, aggressive spread of concrete. Nowadays, the exiting of vehicles requires extra backing and forwarding and backing up again to turn around, but this minor inconvenience is more than made up for in the gain of an area worth lingering in rather than briskly passing through on the way to and from the house.

Plantings of various kinds now encroach on all four sides of the square parking pad. At one side

are pavement beds framed with railroad sleepers merely one course high. The 8-inch (20-cm) depth of soil in the beds has been enough to sustain a small tree (*Weinmannia racemosa*), now 9 feet (2.7 m) tall after two decades in situ, a normal height for a tree of the species in its twenties. The soil has also been sufficient to grow a giant *Astelia* to its full 5 feet (1.5 m) and some of the even taller forms of *Phormium tenax* to their full potential. Plate 20 shows portions of these beds in the early years following their installation, while Plate 21 shows the same beds nearly a quarter century later.

PLATE 20. Pavement beds placed toward the edge of a parking area.

PLATE 19. Sweet woodruff flowers close-up, with a trio of white pansies.

Along another side of the parking pad, lawn, originating as a grass path beyond the edge of the pavement, has been coaxed into creeping over its edge and now forms a 4-foot- (1.2-m-) wide strip of grass carpet on concrete. I've had fun demonstrating my amazing, rollaway grass rug for a few close and indulgent friends, as I will now demonstrate it for you. In Plate 22, the lawn carpet in place. In Plate 23, the lawn carpet rolled up. In my contemplative moments, I realize that this grass-on-concrete hobby of mine is as silly in its way as those 2-foot- (60-cm-) wide handlebar mustaches or 2-foot-long recurving fingernails cultivated by some other extremists.

On a third side of the parking pad stands a grove of Titoki trees (*Alectryon excelsum*) grown tall in two decades, in a 16-inch- (40-cm-) deep pavement bed supported by large boulders (Plate 24). Beneath the trees is a tough, drought-tolerant underplanting of *Agapanthus africanus* (in flower); of a reasonably controllable, tuberless native New Zealand form of the fern *Nephrolepis cordifolia*, that more usually unstoppable spreader; and of several *Neoregelia* bromeliads.

A part of the remaining side of the concrete pad has been richly planted to form something of a hideaway retreat, or at least a resting place where visitors can be half hidden and altogether relaxed. There are two chairs here for a tête-à-tête, and a table for a beverage break. Plate 25, the result of a lucky snapshot, reveals this cozy corner in another use. I say *lucky* because the picture was entirely

PLATE 21. Detail of the "Plate 20" beds a quarter century after planting. In the foreground, variegated *Phormium tenax*. Soil depth is 8 inches (20 cm).

unplanned. Seated at right is my garden friend, Mo Yee, owner of the property. The two little neighbor girls, Brittney and Madison, appeared as suddenly as do certain restless little birds (white eyes and fantails) that also visit the garden, stay but a moment, and then flit away. Expecting as much from this pair, I hastened into the house to get my camera, while Mo, a weaver, wove at the

PLATE 22. Grass lawn, extending over pavement, covers one edge of our paved parking area in Auckland.

PLATE 23. The grass rolls up like a rug.

girls' request, several tiny, spread-winged birds using leaf strips of New Zealand flax (*Phormium tenax*). The girls asked for these weavings to use as decorations on greeting cards they had made at school and would hand to their parents on their wedding anniversary the next day. The girls also asked for a bouquet, which we provided in the form of hydrangeas. This episode represents gardening at its most rewarding.

Plate 26, taken a little to the left of the scene in Plate 25, shows a grouping of table gardens, photographed on another day: three tables at front and in nearly full view, one at the back mostly obscured. Pots of bromeliads with luridly purplish leaves and a potted gardenia (green leaved) hide the table legs. Think of these as elevated pavement

PLATE 24. Groves of Titoki trees (*Alectryon excelsum*) grow on pavement along another edge of our parking pad.

gardens. The gardens on the tables are of diverse themes and unrelated appearance, yet to my eyes at least, they all fit together agreeably, and they certainly add up to a major landscape feature, owing to the uniformity of the tables themselves. If the tables were of various styles, shapes, and sizes, the garden result would be visual chaos. We will look more closely at tabletop gardens in chapters seven and eight.

PLATE 25. A shady retreat fills a corner of our paved parking pad 55 feet (16.8 m) away, and a world apart, from the house.

PLATE 26. Table gardens group at a corner of our concrete parking pad in Auckland.

Up Against Brick Walls

In Plate 27 solid concrete paving runs right up to the base of a 6-foot- (1.8-m-) high brick wall in a shady part of my brother Ken's garden. The question was, How could we bring enlivening plants to this forbidding setting? Container gardening with big plants in tubs or in half-barrels could have been

PLATE 27. Ferns and other forest plants in soil mounded 4 feet (1.2 m) high on pavement, and up against a shady brick wall.

an answer. Yet, pavement gardening seemed a better choice since it would add soft textures—foliages—rather than the hardness of containers to an already hard setting. We decided on a mound garden, and to fashion it we placed composty soil 4 feet (1.2 m) high against the wall, shaping it at its frontal sides into a broad V, sloped back for stability, leveled at its summit. We planted this shaped mound mainly with big, tough, drought-tolerant ferns (*Polystichum, Dryopteris*). There is no armature in the mound of soil, nothing to hold it up except the 45-degree, self-stabilizing slope of its sides, and the roots of the ferns. These have grown vigorously for 4 years, with only occasional watering in times of extended summer dryness.

Plate 28 is a recent picture of the composition taken during fall. Before snapping the camera shutter, I confess that I gussied up the garden by clipping off spent fern fronds—last year's leafage that really should have been removed in springtime. I also thinned out a few perfectly fresh, green fronds—no harm to these vigorous plants—to give the ferns an airier aspect.

Plates 29 and 30 show another example of pavement gardening against a wall: In soil mounded against the shady, north side of a low brick wall abutted by pavement grow the grass *Hakonechloa macra* 'Aureola', the fern *Adiantum pedatum*, and the perennial *Tiarella unifoliata*. The latter, a little-known native of America's West Coast, has evergreen, ground-covering foliage and sparky little white stars that stay for months; it is one of the region's several most garden-worthy

PLATE 28. The "Plate 27" planting 4 years later.

wildflowers. The cap of the wall holds a planting of moss, sedums, and other miniatures beside a bowl of water, an unintended tongue target for the family cats. The massive, splayed leaf at the back of the wall belongs to the controversial garden plant, sometime rash-causing weed *Heracleum*

PLATE 29. Newly set out pavement planting banked against a low brick wall.

mantegazzianum. A biennial or triennial, it is absent from Plate 30, transposed from a photograph taken 2 years later. The against-the-wall planting had by that time grown up to nearly hide the masonry. Moistness of soil (owing to frequent watering) and the coolness of tree shade as well as wall shade have benefited the planting.

Island Plantings

Pavement gardening's reply to the island bed in a grass lawn is the island on pavement. Either of the two compositions requires of the viewer some measure of acceptance of the thing you see as being terra firma arising reassuringly from water rather than from its actual setting. Total acceptance of the illusion would, of course, amount to hallucination and is not to be recommended.

Island plantings on pavement are usually free-form designs that make use of stones or ground covers as shoring rather than milled wood or some other manufactured material as framing. Naturalism in form and material assist in making the island readable as Nature's own. Pavement islands are often little bigger than a sea lion, suiting their placement in small paved areas, but whatever the composition lacks in breadth, it may make up for in height, with a tall planting that provides the island an imposing presence.

PLATE 30. The "Plate 29" planting after 2 years' growth.

Barry's Isle. In Plate 31 sea bluffs shore an island with an apparently misplaced grove of Arizona cypress (*Cupressus arizonica*) at its summit. But allow a little poetic license: As that poet-politician, Senator Barry Goldwater, said of his beloved home state of Arizona, "The desert is our ocean."

PLATE 31. Barry's Isle: A planting of Arizona cypresses (*Cupressus arizonica*) and succulents on a rocky rise.

PLATE 32. *Aloe saponaria* at the base of Barry's Isle, in soil retained by the ground cover *Heterocentron elegans*.

In constructing this high, rocky island, a garden jobber and I stacked some hefty stones, inching the largest of them up a plank, one end of which rested on the pavement, the other end on stones already stacked. We pressed soil into the gaps between the

PLATE 33. Island bed photographed 37 years after planting, with Canadian hemlocks (*Tsuga canadensis* 'Cole's Prostrate') in sections of nineteenth-century city water mains.

rocks as we assembled them, forming plantable crevices. To accommodate the trees at top, we shaped a shallow rock pot with a big, flat stone for the bottom and smaller stones for the sides.

The trees, which were about 10 years old when photographed, have grown slowly on their stony redoubt: the tallest of them stands 42 inches (105 cm). Companion plants, rooted in crevice soil, include the gray-rosetted *Echeveria sucunda*, a miniature reddish *Neoregelia* (*N. chlorostricta* 'Fairy Paint'), various crassulas, *Aloe saponaria* (bottom, at left). At the base of the trees, several species of *Tillandsia*, not rooted in crevices but maintained without soil, are held firmly in place with small stones pressed closely against the scant roots of each plant. The only hardy plants at the party are the trees. If I were to adapt the composition to a garden in a cold region, I might use succulents such as lewisias, sedums, and hardy crassulas.

Feisty but Forgiven. Plate 32 shows a close-up view of the *Aloe saponaria* at the shore of Barry's Isle taken 2 years after the scene of the trees on their rocky height. The *Aloe*, with its 15-inch- (37-cm-) wide rosettes of lizardy-spotted leaves, makes a striking foliage plant for pavement plant-ing. It will grow vigorously in soil only 3 or 4 inches (7.5 or 10 cm) deep, without being watered or otherwise minded much, but it will of course need occasional weeding. Wear gloves. The *Aloe* is armed with business-like barbs along its leaf margins. I, as a weeder, hate this plant, but I, as

a gardener strolling and gazing, admire it enough to always forgive it. Growing at the base of the *Aloe* is the ground cover *Heterocentron elegans*, which has overwhelmed the rocks that I had wedged under the top-heavy *Aloe* rosettes for support years before when planting them. The *Heterocentron* will grow upon and cover garden stones of any size, and will require repeated pruning away from any that you want to keep in view.

Hemlock Isle. In Plate 33 Canadian hemlocks (*Tsuga canadensis* 'Cole's Prostrate') grow where planted 37 years earlier in sections of nineteenth-century city water mains purchased from a dealer

PLATE 35. Bamboo-covered islet or peninsula—however you may see it.

PLATE 34. A rocky isle planting of spear-leaved phormiums and others.

in reclaimed iron. I hired a blacksmith-welder to cut the pipes and join them together. The basal planting features *Campanula poscharskyana* with an ascending stem of violet flowers, sweet alyssum (*Lobularia maritima*) in purple flower, a broad-bladed *Carex* from woods in Maine, and *Sedum album* as a soil retainer in the vicinity of the alyssum. I expect that you will notice my violation of accepted artistry here in the overly muchness of having added flower color to a sculptural composition that would be better with only the green of leaves and the red-brown of rust. And perhaps the minor and neutral whiteness of the *Sedum* when in flower is allowable as well. In fact, during its nearly four decades of existence, the island planting contained no more color than that. The 2 years when I added the violet and purple that you see here amounted to a momentary rebellion against good taste that my more vulgar self thoroughly enjoyed.

In New Zealand. Plate 34 shows spear-leaved *Phormium tenax* 'Burgundy', *P. colensoi* 'Green Dwarf', and the shrublet *Hebe albicans* on an island whose soil is held in place by boulders and the carpeting succulent, *Drosanthemum floribundum*. The bed is no broader than a person's outstretched arms. Yet it is a garden feature of major attraction, arising as it does from the doldrums of an expanse of concrete.

Near Seattle. More of a planting on a peninsula, I suppose, than on an island, the assemblage in Plate

35 of the bamboos *Bambusa ventricosa* (tallest) and *Sasa palmata* (low-growing, with broad leaves) and the ground-covering perennial *Campanula poscharskyana* grows entirely on pavement but can't be circumnavigated (as any sure-enough island will allow). The rustic rocker sets a deceiving scale: the chair is actually child-size.

In Tropical Highland. In Plate 36 three tree ferns (*Cibotium*) grow in a crescent-shaped island bed 10 feet (3 m) long, 3 feet (90 cm) wide, 17 inches (43 cm) high, retained with unmortared stones—quarried granite, angular and chunky. Two helpers and I had no difficulty setting up nearly smooth walls with these stones. The filling of the bed with soil came last, after the stonework and after the placing of the "trees" in the bed.

We planted tree ferns that were about 15 to 18 years old, with trunks more or less as tall as grown people and a weight of about 150 pounds (75 kg) each after we had bare-rooted them and cut off all their fronds in preparation for trucking the trees to the garden site. Instead of guying their trunks with wires, we braced them with big, heavy pieces of granite placed about their root balls, well below soil level in the island bed, and out of sight. A full complement of splendid new fronds began developing within weeks after the planting.

Tree ferns form a dense mass of roots that tend to out-muscle all but the toughest of plantings at the fern's base. Among the most resilient plants we've used here as underlings are *Cymbidium* orchids, along with *Neoregelia* and *Aechmea* bromeliads. These carry on untrammeled by rooty tree ferns, and flower well in the filmy shade of

PLATE 36. Tree ferns (*Cibotium*) in an island bed retained with dry stone edging.

PLATE 37. Mossy seating at a corner of the tree fern island.

their fronds. Tree fern shade is perfect for these plants and inviting to people. There the great ferns stand, waving a come-hither as sirenically as coconut palms on some island paradise, a port of call complete—to tell the whole truth and cut the smarm—with awesome poverty, muggers, and incurable viruses. Is there any getaway out there as good as the garden at home? Well, yes. But for me, no.

Soft as Down. An edge of the tree fern island, cushioned with moss, serves as seating (Plate 37). If I'm expecting garden visitors, I'll wait to water the island bed until after they've gone, or will tend to the watering the evening before the garden date so that the moss will have a chance to dry and not dampen any posteriors. But sometimes on a warm day I'll sit here alone on damp moss, blissfully unbothered, what the heck.

Spontaneous Pavement Plantings

Pavement planting takes place spontaneously when plants that grow beside pavement spill over its surface. The gardener either welcomes the growth as a garden improvement, or deplores the spillover as disorderly and prunes it back. In one of my own gardens, the setting has seemed to call for the formal shaping of plants used as pavement garden edging, and here I've been a hard-line pruner (Plate 13), but mainly I'm a welcomer of the over-the-pavement excursions of plants. The enhancement of gardens by this flow of foliage has never, I believe, been adequately recognized and commended. When pavement-side plantings are allowed to burgeon outward to a reasonable extent, the effect on the landscape is that of fulfillment and prosperity: One's garden cup runneth over, with a tangible joy in living that is readily transferable from plants to people.

But first determine whether or not this easeful growth suits the style of the garden, then decide on the reasonable extent to which such casual

PLATE 38. A walkway teeming with plants leads into woods.

leafiness may be allowed to proceed, and keep hedge loppers handy: This big scissors for two-hand use is the best tool I've found for the pruning back. In my own gardening, though, the restraints I place upon the spontaneous pavement plants I live with are, in most areas, lenient in the extreme. I enjoy having plants greet me by tapping me on the shoulder or by gently whisk-brooming my trouser legs as I pass by; as long as I can make my way through, the plants encroaching on my walkways seem to me perfectly in place. The amazing grass rug that has woven itself over a concrete pad in our Auckland garden, and which I maintain in shamelessly puerile fascination, is one such example (see Plates 22 and 23).

Back Dooryard. Plates 38 and 39 show the walkway and steps near our back door in Auckland. We encourage this evident chumminess with our plants; both we and they gain from it. Unless a person is unusually preoccupied while walking to or from the door, it is hard not to notice some plant that has good news, or some other that needs attention. The plants banking the walkway include *Neoregelia*, Vireya rhododendrons, *Cymbidium*, *Crassula multicava*, *Adiantum*, *Plectranthus coleoides*, and *Canna hortensis* 'Phasion' with its tiger-striped leaves. Lacing the risers of the steps are an English ivy of uncertainly minor form (*Hedera helix* 'Minima'), Kenilworth ivy (*Cymbalaria muralis*), and baby's tears (*Soleirolia soleirolii*).

Front Dooryard. On the way to and from our front door in Auckland, we enjoy the companionship of a Dalmatian wildflower of cliff faces,

PLATE 39. Back dooryard with chummy plants.

Campanula portenschlagiana. Shown in Plate 40 with a lone, out-of-season stem of flowers, the plant turns into a blue-violet glory in springtime. This species used to be called—would that it still were—*C. muralis*, which translates as the campanula of walls. True to that name, the plant has climbed from a bed at top, down over the brick wall, and has taken root in scant, naturally accumulating leaf mold in corners of the concrete steps at bottom.

PLATE 40. Front door steps made personable with plants.

The waterlily in view, which grows in a 2-inch (5-cm) depth of mud, with an equal depth of water above, is the 'Alba' form of the European *Nymphaea pygmaea*. It has been in its bowl for 2 years (here in our almost-always frost-free garden) without a change of soil, and with no trouble except the hatching out of mosquito wigglers, easily controlled without harm to the plant by spraying a little pyrethrum on the water surface (an anti-mosquito treatment equally effective in the water tanks of bromeliad leaves). Any time now I intend to tip the *Nymphaea* out of its bowl, wash its roots with the garden hose, and replant it in fresh soil.

Other plants in the bed at the back include the fern *Doodia media*, native to Pacific Islands from New Zealand north to Hawaii. This fern "flowers" splendidly when its new fronds unfurl, rose-bronze in color, during springtime rains. In faux-flower here for months is the Brazilian bromeliad *Nidularium regelioides*, with its rosy bull's-eye of small, bract-like inner leaves centering a rosette of big, glossy green strap leaves.

Scented Walking. Follow the yellow brick road in Plate 41 and you may expect, as you brush your way through, to be spritzed by plants with piquant aromas. Among them are Jerusalem sage (*Phlomis fruticosa*) at lower left, lemon balm (*Melissa officinalis*), and other scented herbs—all of them friendly and forward in growth. The path is located in North Vancouver's Park and Tilford Garden.

PLATE 41. Jerusalem sage (*Phlomis fruticosa*) at lower left; lemon balm (*Melissa officinalis*) and other scented herbs along a brick path—closely enough that you savor their aromas in brushing by.

PLATE 42. Thyme lawn tiding across steps, photographed during sunset with its long shadows and gold suffusion. Photo by Robert E. Major.

Thyme Steps. Twenty-some years before the scene in Plate 42 was photographed in my Finn Hill garden near Seattle, I had planted several named selections of mother of thyme (*Thymus praecox* subsp. *arcticus*) beside the steps. Bees hybridized these plants; vigorous hybrid seedlings overgrew and supplanted their parents, and spread out over pavement as you see. After two decades in place this hybrid swarm of thyme on pavement has built up a sod of humus several inches deep beneath its stems. The footsteps of pedestrians prune the plants, keeping them from growing where they would interfere with foot traffic. No other pruning has ever been done.

PLATE 43. A 6-year-old Mexican daisy (*Erigeron karvinskianus*) has crept across the lower step in the garden of Leonard and Katie Baker. Seen here in mid-October, the plant is full of flowers from spring until fall frost.

Daisy Steps. In the Bakers' garden in North Vancouver, Leonard does the tidying, Katie the planting. Four years before Plate 43 was photographed, Katie planted *Erigeron karvinskianus* in soil at the side of the steps. The plant has marched all the way across, rooting in mere dust that has collected beneath it. Leonard shears the branch growth once a year in early spring to keep the plant compact. This little pink-and-white daisy, native to Mexican mountains (hardy in zone 5), is one of the world's nicest weeds for garden use on pavement or dry rocks; it flowers all through summer and well into autumn. I've always thought of this daisy as the Royal Britannic vagabond among garden plants, for it has immigrated just about everywhere the British have settled; it has come and escaped from gardens, and naturalized on wild crags. I find it on outcroppings in suburban Victoria, British Columbia, and in Auckland, New Zealand. If I ever get to India, I'll expect to find it there on rocks, as I do elsewhere, aswarm with butterflies and hover flies, a helpful and apparently harmless addition to the regional ecology.

Burly Tropicals. In our lowland tropical garden on Samar Island (Plate 44), a walkway of dressed limestone blocks is cozied by plantings of a big hybrid *Neoregelia* bromeliad (deplorably named Maiden's Blush) at lower left; of dark green *Rhoeo spathacea* and pea-green *Pilea microphylla*, both plants at the center of the scene. At the upper right, *Pandanus dubius* brandishes its broad sword leaves atop a dry stone wall.

PLATE 44. Tropicals in the author's garden on Samar Island.

CHAPTER FOUR

On Stepping Stones, Parking Grids, and Pavers

Plantings in any of the three garden features named in the chapter title above are to be chosen for their allowance of being stepped on. Some such plants are more accommodating than others, and their various tolerances are noted in the final section of this chapter, Paver Plants.

Planted Stepping Stones

PLATE 45. Stepping stone walkway immediately after planting. Somewhat stark and edgy just now, but give the plants a couple of years to fill out and become comradely.

A garden walkway of stepping stones brought to life with an accompanying planting of ground covers often becomes one of the garden's most attractive features, or even the central feature that unites all else in view. The journey proposed by such stones with their planting is so coaxing that only hopelessly preoccupied people could turn away without walking the walk, if not on foot, then visually, with a slow beguiled gaze.

Stepping Stones Newly Planted. The new planting in Plate 45 appears raw and unsettled, less than beguiling as yet, but I believe you can see what it is going to become in time and with care. Use your powers of foresight to visualize all these plants united in growth, a full tapestry of foliages with no soil showing. Or, if you prefer a less bounding garden, let a little bare soil remain between the various clump-forming perennials that grow beside the stones. The future, as you see, will turn this stark assemblage of plants, recently liberated from pots, gallons (4 liters), and 5-gallon (20-liter) containers, into—yes—a beguiling stroll through beds of established perennials.

PLATE 46. Slabs of granite form a stepping stone way in the garden of Dan and Susan Nelson. Blue star creeper (*Laurentia fluviatilis*) covers soil between the stones, and silvery, grass-like tufts of *Carex comans* 'Frosted Curls' thrust upward from the ground cover.

The ground cover between the stones is blue star creeper (*Laurentia fluviatilis*) ex 4-inch (10-cm) pots, set out in springtime at about 18-inch (46-cm) intervals. These potlings will need at least two summers to grow into a full cover. For cover in one summer the garden jobbers who installed this planting would have had to use twice the number of blue star creepers, centering them about 9 inches (23 cm) apart. This species is one of the more rapidly spreading and more steppable stepping stone plants, a good choice for this garden where it is the only ground cover between the stones. In some other paver gardens containing a variety of ground covers or alpine tufts, blue star might readily turn into a little death star, invading by means of stolons any other low-growing plant in its way. Much less invasive but equal to blue star creeper in speed of growth and in traffic resistance are *Acaena, Herniaria,* and various thymes listed in the plant descriptions at the end of this chapter.

Granite Stones, Carpeting Plants. A stepping stone pathway in the garden of Dan and Susan Nelson journeys through a planting of blue star creeper (*Laurentia fluviatilis*) growing closely about the stones (Plate 46). Companion foliages and flowers include the silvery, grass-like *Carex comans* 'Frosted Curls' (synonym *C. albula*), a hybrid *Fuchsia* and, in white flower, sweet alyssum (*Lobularia maritima*), an annual that often self-sows.

Mossy Landing. At a stopping place along the Nelsons' stepping stone way, gardener Barbara Barry has planted, in between the stones, collected clumps of the moss *Leptobryum pyriforme*

(Plate 47). Toward the back of the scene, the ground cover *Acaena microphylla* flows up harmlessly about the ornamental grass *Pennisetum orientale*.

Don't Tread on Me. Plate 48 features a lush planting of baby's tears (*Soleirolia soleirolii*) at the edge of a flagstone terrace on the shady side of the Nelsons' home. Foot traffic, anathema to baby's tears, has curtailed the growth of the ground cover along its front edge. Rex begonias and ferns grow in the background.

PLATE 47. A true moss (*Leptobryum pyriforme*) grows between stepping stones. The ground cover *Acaena microphylla* and a clump-forming grass, *Pennisetum orientale*, complete the composition.

PLATE 48. Baby's tears (*Soleirolia soleirolii*) and rex begonias edge the flagstones at the shady side of the Nelsons' home.

The Planting of Parking Grids

Plantable concrete grids as an alternative to solid paving are a German invention introduced in the mid-twentieth century. Since then the idea has caught on in many countries and is in use on countless thousands of properties. The system provides a grid of concrete that can be driven over and parked upon, while providing interspaces that will support plants whose mass presence will reduce the runoff of rain storms, and whose exhalations will cool the air during hot weather (a blessed relief from vicious, heat-radiating acreages of asphalt), while oxygenating the air at all times. The apertures in the gridwork are usually not filled with soil, thereby leaving space in which plants grow essentially protected from vehicles.

Lawn grasses sown over the installed gridwork are the more usual kind of planting. Grass lawn is at its best in a loamy soil beneath the grids that is native to the site. A superimposed soil mix of the usual airy texture might render

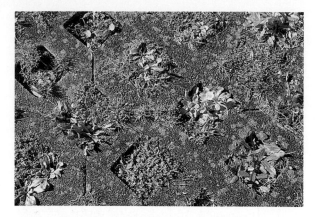

PLATE 49. Good-looking weeds and mosses have filled unplanted spaces in this parking area gridwork.

PLATE 50. Gridwork planting of herb baron (*Thymus herba-barona*) in flower and of *Rubus calycinoides*.

grid paving unstable, even if the mix were well compacted after being spread. Grid-lawns on home properties easily survive being driven on several times daily; but parking on grid-grass for more than a few hours at a time, amounting to more than a dozen or so hours a week, will weaken and thin the grass beneath the vehicle's chassis and kill the grass beneath its tires.

Grid-covered parking areas are quite often not planted, in which case Nature supplies the gridwork with vagrant plants, often in rich array; and these weeds will perform all the good work of a grass lawn in the same situation—but not where parked upon for long. Not even the toughest weeds will prosper where vehicles stand frequently for an extended time.

As a connoisseur of weeds, I find rich visual pickings in the interlopers that occupy unplanted grid paving. In Plate 49 are just a few of the eleven kinds of weeds that hold the fort in a certain grid-work weed patch. They are subjected only rarely to parking. Therefore, they are doing wonderfully well. The owner of the weed-haven runs a lawn mower over it every 2 weeks during the growing season, inadvertently keeping the weeds as neatly compact as choice alpines.

That particular weed garden grows amid grids of one of the older styles. In one of the newer models, the plantable apertures are bigger and most of the concrete is below ground (Plate 50). The area is a part of the garden of a condominium apartment building where movers' vans park only occasionally. The grids were laid here on a leveled expanse of clayey soil. A bedding mix mainly of compost was spread over the installed grids to a depth of several inches, leaving less than 2 inches (5 cm) of the grids' concrete posts uncovered. This shallow space between soil surface and post tops offers the plants only slight protection from tires. Even so, the combination parking area–ground cover garden succeeds because of the infrequency of its use for parking. The planting includes scattered clumps of the ornamental grass *Pennisetum orientale* (not in the picture) near the edges of the gridded area where tires will probably never touch it. The plants in view are *Thymus herba-barona* (fine of leaf) and *Rubus calycinoides* (broad-leaved). The herb-baron will recover easily from being driven over. The *Rubus* will be skinned and mashed by truck tires but will recover in time; yet, this rampageous species seems a questionable choice for grid gardening. *Waldsteinia fragarioides* (included in chapter two's list of soil-holding and frame-covering plants) would lend the same broad-leaf contrast to the fine leaves in this planting as that provided by the *Rubus*, without that plant's invasiveness and frequent need of pruning.

Planting between Patio Pavers

Ground cover plantings in the seams of pavers are relatively high-maintenance garden features that are well worth the effort. Be prepared though for the need to weed by hand several times a year, slow work—and expensive if you have it done. It is a task made doubly taxing by the need to winkle the weeds carefully from between the ground cover's branches, minimizing damage. Among the most devilish and triumphant weeds in this situation are wild grass seedlings. I've tried a liquid grass killer which supposedly kills grass selectively without much harm to other plants. I used it several times during one growing season and found that, while it did not kill grass outright, at least it set back grass growth considerably. Then I gave up using the toxin ever again. Enough moaning. Here is the good part: the charm of ground covers as pavement garments of unique textures. Trodden upon, some of these plants (the thymes) release delightful aromas, and all are great toe ticklers if you will go forth boldly with bare feet.

PLATE 51. Paver planting underway: the plug of gray foliage bears the name *Thymus pseudolanuginosus*.

PLATE 52. The "Plate 51" planting after a year's growth.

the sand on which the concrete slabs had been placed. The slabs at 1½ inches (4 cm) apart are too close for easy planting in between, but are perhaps at the maximum safe distance apart: Wider spacing might catch the heels of shoes. I gave up trying to plant the inch- (2.5-cm-) wide seams between many of the slabs. The sand won't nourish the ground covers, but the plants will soon send roots down into subsoil beneath, and Nancy's gardeners will keep the planting moist and fertilized during its touchy first summer.

Plate 52 shows the same plants as in Plate 51, a year and a month later. They now measure about 1 foot (30 cm) in their longer dimension. The sand in which these thymes grow has discouraged seedling grasses and other weeds and has eased the removal of the few weeds that have cropped up.

Planting Underway. Plate 51 shows a newly laid terrace at the home of my garden friend Nancy D. Short in western Washington State. For the planting, I had purchased a variety of finely textured ground covers in 4-inch (10-cm) pots. In view here are *Thymus* 'Pink Chintz', planted, and *T. pseudolanuginosus*, about to be. I've used a kitchen knife to divide each pot plant into two to four pieces, depending on the plant's relative fullness of growth, and have used the same stout blade to scrape, between the pavers, planting trenches in

By the Sea. A patio serves as a visual and physical landing pad in any garden that has one. In the seaside garden designed and planted by Suzanne Pocock (in collaboration with Mary Fisher of Cultus Bay Nursery)—a garden for Sue, for her husband, Stanley, and for ourselves as visitors—are two patios, two persuasive invitations to tarry. Both patios have been made of slabs of Pennsylvania blue sandstone interplanted with ground covers.

The stone is far too sightly to be concealed beneath broadly spreading mat plants. By trial and error Sue has found ground covers with the perfect tact for the job. In the interspaces of the patio at the property's entry grows New Zealand's *Cotula perpusilla* 'Platt's Black', a dark purplish selection of a plant species also available in a silvery gray form. In Sue's planting the *Cotula*, after two summers of growth, has richly embroidered the crevices in which it was planted but hasn't ventured over the stones at all, exactly to the satisfaction of the gardener (Plate 53). Background shrubs planted near the edge of this patio include *Hydrangea quercifolia* and *Fuchsia magellanica* 'Versicolor Variegata', photographed 9 August in full flower, the hydrangea ivory white, the fuchsia classically fuchsine in color.

In the other patio, at the beach side of the house (Plate 54), grow two kinds of thyme, one good and one bad in Sue's reckoning which is based on the plants' relative powers of growth. The good guy is a dwarf form of creeping thyme, *Thymus praecox* 'Elfin', which covers stone by inches; the bad actor (but only so on this stage) is woolly thyme, *T. pseudolanuginosus*, which covers by the foot (30 cm) and yard (90 cm). Sue has been tearing out the stronger grower and replacing it little by little with plugs of the 'Elfin' thyme, whenever it spreads enough to allow harvesting. The only remaining part of the woolly thyme is at the patio's far edge as shown in the color plate—the gray plant near a sculpturesque block of driftwood. Woolly thyme's determination to cover mineral surfaces, a talent unappreciated here, is a downright thrill to those of us with naked pavement we want clothed. (See Plate 55 for a close-up view of this plant as a great couturier of concrete.)

A brief pathway leads from the Pococks' beachside patio to the shore, a track of native beach sand windrowed and wave-rowed here long ago and well firmed by time and conglomeration. The same sand supports the patio stones and has in time, with the decay of shoreline vegetation, acquired enough humus to be a nutritious garden medium. Plants of *Euphorbia cyparissias* (yellow flowers on stems of gray needle leaves, soft to touch) and of a purple-leaved and -flowered form of *Sedum telephium* near the edge of the patio increase as vigorously in this sand as do the patio's mat plants. The *Euphorbia* can be an invasive spreader by stolons but won't menace the equally strong *Sedum* in this garden community. Beyond

PLATE 53. *Cotula perpusilla* 'Platt's Black' richly embroiders the seams between these paving stones but hardly covers their top surfaces.

PLATE 55. *Thymus pseudolanuginosus* has spread 3 feet (90 cm) across pavement in 5 years. This planting by Katie Baker includes lady's mantle (*Alchemilla vulgaris*) in midsummer flower.

these low growers, at the far side of the path, Sue has planted ornamental grasses that blend easily with the seaside thicket of indigenous reeds.

Totemic sculptures rise from this thicket; the carvings are a retirement hobby of our host. Stan's working life has been spent in what must be one of the rarest professions: He is a fourth-generation

PLATE 54. Planted patio at seaside. The principal paver plant is *Thymus praecox* 'Elfin', chosen for its minor ability to cover stones too good-looking to be concealed entirely.

builder of racing shells whose company has supplied university rowing teams across America. So, he has always worked with wood. His totem people intrigue me, as a curator of tribal sculptures in a faraway museum, for the stylistic kinship they bear with certain figurated posts and panels carved by tribesmen in the northern mountains of the Philippines. These sculptures have not been exported or published; to know them you would have to go to the Philippines, which Stan has not yet done. I see no mystery though in their translocation into his front yard. They seem to be universal ancestral figures visualized by the tom-tom tribal who is more or less active within us all. Count on the seaside to bring out this other self who counsels some of us in our artistry, including of course garden art, and turns many others among us into that fairly harmless form of hunter and gatherer, the beachcomber.

Paver Plants

Plants listed here are flat-growing perennials or shrublets that will withstand much, some, or a little foot traffic when they are planted in the seams of flagstone pavers, or between sections of poured pavement from which the board dividers have been pulled. The plants will grow forth from these narrow places and partly cover the mineral surfaces. The plants' varying durability when trodden upon is indicated by a code: Traffic 1, for the most durable kinds; traffic 2, for those somewhat durable; traffic 3, for those that don't like being walked on at all but will survive an occasional trodding. Of all these plants, only *Cotula* will tolerate slow-draining soil; the rest require rapid drainage, as for alpine plants, which many of them *are* natively. The hardiness of each plant is indicated in a numerical system adapted from that of United States Department of Agriculture. The lower the number the hardier the plant: Zones 1, 2, 3, and 4 indicate hardiness well below 0°F (−18°C); zones 5 and 6, hardiness below but near 0°F (−18°C); zone 7, hardiness just above 0°F (−18°C). (But local conditions alter the hardiness of plants.)

Acaena buchananii. Zone 4. One of the most traffic-resistant carpeting plants. Has been used in its native New Zealand to cover the soil of a rural airfield. Inch- (2.5-cm-) long leaves, silky gray, toothed, and divided like those of roses to which the acaenas are related. Best in sun. Traffic 1.

Acaena microphylla. Zone 5. A bronzy leaved mat whose rounded flower heads with their long red spines resemble sea urchins. Clip off the showy flowers when they fade. If left to go to seed they become the kind of stick-tights that will attack your socks. Sun or part shade. Traffic 2.

Arenaria verna. Irish moss (kelly green) and Scotch moss (yellow-green). Zone 2. The two color forms of the plant are indeed moss-like in growth, mounding, and minute of leaf, but unlike moss, they bears flowers, white and sequin-like in their tininess and closeness on the fabric of the plant. Irish moss (Plate 56) and Scotch moss are among the most popular paver and stepping stone plants, but they are touchy, sometimes dying out after several years in place. No fault of the gardener; some kind of blight, probably incurable, is the culprit. Sun or part shade. Traffic 2.

***Calluna vulgaris* 'Dainty Bess Minor'.** Zone 3. A frosty-appearing, gray-green mound, this miniature Scotch heather grows to about 3 inches (7.5 cm) high and a foot (30 cm) across. Lavender flowers in summer. Give it sun. Traffic 3.

Cotula squalida. Zone 4. A mat of small, dark green ferny leaves. Best in sun; a shady location loosens its growth. Spreads just a little over pavement, usually less than a foot (30 cm) away from its rooting point in a paver's seam. This species is hardly circumspect, however, when it comes up against other paver plants, which it will invade and likely overwhelm. Other cotulas of smaller leaf and denser habit than that of *C. squalida* have never in my gardening experience invaded other plants. Neither do they cover pavement at all, but they make gorgeous leafy embroidery along the paver seams in which they are planted. Two of these good little *Cotula* species are **C. minor**, bright green of leaf, and **C. perpusilla**, marketed in at least two forms, one dark purple, the other, grayish with a metallic sheen—a form that my garden friend Nancy D. Short describes as being "like silver velvet," there in between the pavement blocks of her patio. All three species are serviceable in traffic 2.

PLATE 56. A 5-year-old plant of Irish moss (*Arenaria verna*) extends a foot-and-a-half (45 cm) over the backyard patio of Leonard and Katie Baker. The plant is pictured in full, midsummer flower—a sprinkling of white dots. Companions include lavender-flowered *Thymus vulgaris*, yellow *Sedum acre*, and pink *Rosa* 'Ballerina'.

Dianthus gratianopolitanus 'Tiny Rubies'. Zone 3. A low mound of blue-gray foliage, to a foot (30 cm) across. Rosy flowers in early summer. Likes sun. Other selections or hybrids of *D. gratianopolitanus* are usable as paver plants, as is the separate species, *D. arvernensis*. Traffic 2.

Dryas octopetala. Zone 1. A flat-growing shrub with gray-green scalloped leaves suggesting those of oak trees, but only an inch (2.5 cm) long. White anemone-like flowers in early summer, followed by silvery, long-tailed seeds in globular arrangement. For sunny pavers, on which it will grow 2 feet (60 cm) or more across. *Dryas octopetala* 'Minor' is the same plant, except for being half-size in its leaves and growth. Traffic 3.

Frankenia capitata 'Leavis' and *F. thymifolia*. Zone 4. Tiny gray leaves and starry pink summer flowers in flat, wiry-branched mats. Best in sun. Traffic 1.

Herniaria glabra. Zone 2. One of the tiniest in leaf and densest in growth of any paver plant. Lentil-size green leaves that redden with winter sun. Takes sun or shade. Traffic 1.

Laurentia fluviatilis. Blue star creeper. Zone 6. A spread of little dull green leaves, as flat as can be where stepped on. Good show of light blue star flowers in summer. Invasive of any other low plants that it comes up against. Sun or half shade. Traffic 1.

Phlox subulata. Moss pink. Zone 1. Many named forms—pink, white, parti-colored, rose- or magenta-flowered—are in the nursery trade. All

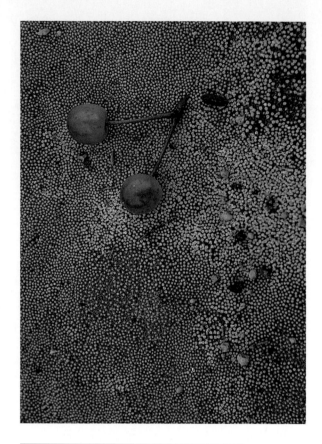

PLATE 57. Detail of *Raoulia lutescens*, as a paver plant. Twin Montmorency cherries set the scale of the raoulia's minute yellow flowers produced closely against a dense, yellow-green mat of equally minute leaves. Photo by Robert E. Major.

make low, dense mounds of tiny needle-form leaves. They prefer sun and are suited to the less trodden areas of paving. Traffic 3.

Raoulia australis. Zone 5. Minute, silvery-gray leaves densely packed in a broadly spreading mat. Garden visitors of mine who have never seen this plant before have thought they were looking at a piece of cloth someone dropped. Tiny yellow button-form flowers in early spring. *Raoulia lutescens* is a yellowish-green mat (Plate 57), smaller and slower in growth than *R. australis*. **Raoulia tenuicaulis**, olive green with glints of silver, makes wider growth at a faster rate than that of the other two. In early spring, it opens tiny, pale yellow flowers whose opiate sweetness is detectable many feet downwind. All three raoulias need sun and are hardy to zone 5. Traffic 2.

Scleranthus biflorus. Zone 5. A bright, light green mound, widening into a mat; minute yellow flowers. In appearance much like the arenarias in this list, and also like those plants in sometimes dying out for no apparent reason. Sun or part shade. Traffic 2.

Soleirolia soleirolii. Baby's tears. Zone 7. Best planted in an untrodden area of pavers; this plant would much prefer never being stepped on. It happens, however, that I have it growing, where it seeded itself, on pavement walked on constantly. Baby's tears has here become compacted to a quarter inch (6 mm) in height and grows slowly. In easier places the plant grows rapidly, forming an airy froth of pea-green, pinhead-size leaves held 4

inches (10 cm) or more high on fragile stems (see Plate 48). For full shade or filtered shade. Traffic 3.

Thymus. Thyme. Zone 5 without snow cover; zone 2 where covered with snow. Several species and varieties of thyme rank among the best of carpeters for planting between pavers. Highly recommended are **T. doerfleri**, **T. 'Doreta Klaber'**, **T. 'Pink Chintz'**, **T. pseudolanuginosus**, and any of the more vigorous "*serpyllum*" (*T. praecox* subsp. *arcticus*) varieties. The thymes prefer sun and heat but grow well (if taller and more open) in half shade. Honeybees are mad for the early summer flowers of these plants (except that *T. pseudolanuginosus* flowers sparingly or not at all). Traffic 2.

Veronica pectinata. Zone 2. A mat of little, felted, gray-green leaves rounded like a gerbil's ears but with notches on the rim (Plate 109, the curtain plant descending from the edge of the table garden). Showy spring flowers, deep blue with a white eye, or, in the variety **'Rosea'**, as named. Best in sun. Traffic 3.

CHAPTER FIVE

On Rocks and Railings

Nature is an eternal rock gardener. In Plate 58 we see a dome of granite in Canadian mountains, shaped by the grinding action of a glacier during the Ice Age of about ten thousand years ago. The gardening of the scoured rock began with the arrival of lichens and of moss, which still inhabit the rock in extensive patches. The aging and flaking away of portions of both primitive plants has supplied fissures in the rock face with humus into which huckleberries and alpine conifers have seeded, and into which they now add their own mulch of dropped parts.

PLATE 58. Moss, shrubs, and trees have seeded themselves on this dome of glaciated granite. Such natural rock-top vegetation has informed the arts of bonsai and rock gardening.

The conifers have grown slowly into trees much smaller than those of the same age in deep soil, standing tall where you see them at the background of the scene. Rock-top trees in exposed

---

PLATE 59. Self-sown hemlocks (*Tsuga mertensiana*) with bonsai character built in them by a hard life on a cliff, trees several decades old but only a foot (30 cm) tall, crampon-rooted on tiny shelves of stone.

positions such as this (see also Plate 59), where they are pummeled and gnarled by wind and drifting snow, dwarfed by a life in scant soil, are the sort whose stressed form and indomitable spirit have inspired the art of bonsai. In one of this chapter's segments, bonsai are released from their pots and returned to a life on rocks as their natural home.

Viewed from another intellectual perspective, Plate 58 shows a rough balance of rock and of plant life in Nature, an equality I believe to be soothing to many of us, a satisfying unity of our softer world of foliages and our harder one of mineral. Gardeners in the British Isles during the Victorian and Edwardian eras were enough taken with this marriage of plants and rocks that they invented rock gardening based on such natural example.

The art is far more often the growing of plants beside rocks than on top, although some carpeting plants will engulf any nearby rocks. Deliberate planting on top of rocks deserves to be more popular in that it offers platform gardening's special rewards: Small plants viewed closer to eye level are easier to tend and enjoy, and all plants are pleasantly surprising, a little mystifying, for being up off the main ground, and are apparently pleased with themselves for being there. It is enough for them to have 1 or 2, or 6 or 8 inches (2.5 or 5, or 15 or 20 cm) of soil to root in, soil depth depending on plant variety. The rest of it is routine horticulture, the provision of water (as often as daily in dry weather) and fertilizer (in liquid form, perhaps twice a month, or once every couple of months during the growing season, depending on one's own enthusiasm for fertilizing). Those are the simple basics of gardening well atop rocks.

Rock-top Tours

Rock-top gardens can be created on individual rocks, on dry stone and mortared stone structures, and atop the railings of concrete (Plate 60) or brick walls. Examples of these possibilities follow here.

Docile Sempervivums, Fierce Yucca. Native to European mountains, sempervivums are designed for a life on rocks, as shown here in our garden near Seattle (Plate 61). For years these colonies have hunkered on their rock as contentedly as cows in clover. As for the rock, it is the size of a large refrigerator and weighs 4 tons. When we hauled it here from the Cascade Mountains, with the sanction of a U.S. Forest Service permit, and hoisted it off the side of the truck using a cable and crane arm, the truck's tires on the opposite side rose high into the air and remained there until the rock touched ground. Whew! Planted on this rock, in a 2-inch (5-cm) depth of soil, the sempervivums thrive with little care aside from watering about twice weekly during droughty summer weather. While sempervivums are drought-tolerant, I don't let them become overly dry. Dryish is all right, but complete dryness will stop their growth and if continued too long will prove fatal.

Companion plants growing beside the rock include the rapier-leaved *Yucca glauca*, with the shrub *Mahonia nervosa* covering ground at its base. I dug the *Yucca* from where it grew wild on the cattle ranch of a friend located in Montana; there the needle-tipped foliage of the plant is as safe from grazing beef as it was from the bison. Here

PLATE 60. The epiphyte *Collospermum hastatum*, with its corn-ear-like flowers, is here growing directly on top of a high wall, where it was placed about 10 years earlier, with nothing more than a peck of composty soil and a couple of rocks to brace it. The wall retains a garden uphill.

in the garden the *Yucca* is a sneaky stabber of hands and forearms every time I try to weed beneath it or prune away its old dead leaves, as I've been doing now for 30 years. Whenever we go into combat, the *Yucca* and I, blood is let—mine—a few drops at a time. Gloves are no help and neither is any jacket I've ever worn.

I've never seriously considered practicing on this *Yucca* (for which I have a grudging fondness, since we've been through so much together) a drastic technique I've hit upon for neutralizing any of the armed yuccas: clipping off the needle tip of every leaf on the plant. I've done this with a *Yucca americana* that I grow in another garden. That plant, too, had been spiking me mercilessly. *Yucca* needles are as hard as iron wood, I've discovered, and getting them off requires a firm squeeze with a heavy-duty pair of hand clippers (secateurs). But I have pangs of conscience about this operation, reckoning that it is marked at some point on a scale of reprehensibility that also registers the pulling of the teeth and claws of a carnival lion. The *Yucca* is another gorgeously fierce creature undeserving of being disarmed for human convenience.

Rock-top Bonsai. My experiments in growing bonsai directly on rocks have come about because of my slowly developing dissatisfaction with cultivating the trees in regular bonsai pots. I've grown and trained bonsai ever since becoming fascinated with them while touring Japan in 1958. The dictates of modesty should deter me from adding, but the jaybird of pride and joy compels me to say, that lately the best of my trees, a Sitka spruce (*Picea sitchensis*) that I've been working on since 1964, has been accepted as a donation to the Pacific Rim Bonsai Collection. Mr. De Groot, the curator of that splendid public display, deems the spruce worthy of being shown in rotation with (ahem)

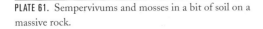

PLATE 61. Sempervivums and mosses in a bit of soil on a massive rock.

PLATE 62. A pre-bonsai in a snazzy pot.

other masterpieces of bonsai art. This same tree is also on display, none too clearly, toward the background of Plate 86, as a bonsai growing on rock. In the foreground of that picture is a grove of maples also growing on a rock, the same trees that my sharp-eyed reader will find, as shown on another page, growing by other means, in another garden, in a more recent year.

Up until the 1990s I grew my trees mainly in imported Japanese pots made for the purpose. Beautifully styled, rigidly stylized, the very soul of old Japan manifested in clay, these pots, I have come to realize, are totally out of place in my suburban garden in Washington State, with its stylistic

PLATE 63. The "Plate 62" treelet liberated from pot life.

origins in England, in the Pacific Northwest wilderness, and in my own notions. First, I tried replacing Japanese pots with the plainest of undecorated and unglazed Italian and Mexican terracotta. In these containers, of no regional definition, my trees appeared measurably more compatible with my garden. The improvement was, as I say, measurable, but not great. Then I thought, How about no pots at all, just a rock base for the tree roots? Would it work? Could the trees be kept moist enough without the cupping of pottery about their roots?

I tried it, placing some of my trees on flat, or reasonably flat stones, with as much or more soil

about their roots as they had had in their pots. I've covered the soil-and-root mass of each bonsai, now on a rock and surrounded by air, with an insulating blanket of moss or other fine ground cover. Water requirements (daily in dry weather) have been no more than for bonsai growing in pots. My rock-top bonsai seem to me considerably bettered, relaxed, more akin to the still-forested region in which I garden and even to the forested world at large. In October each year I lift the trees off their rocks (or ask to have it done if I'm away) and heel them into a sawdust bed for the winter. The trees are returned to their rocks in the spring, after any danger of deep frost.

The ideal stone for the base of a bonsai is flat enough on its underside that it does not teeter when placed on a table or railing, flat enough on its upper side to hold soil about the tree's roots in all quarters, and broad enough to provide a couple of inches of rock surface outside the soil mass all around the tree. The extra surface helps the tree to appear secure and at ease on its rock, a nice but not crucial feature. An advantage, not a necessity, is gained by employing a stone with a basin on its top side into which the tree's roots will fit, but any such depression must be imperfect enough to allow water to drain from it.

In our Auckland garden I've planted, on a stone of the imperfect basin type, a small *Picea glauca* 'Conica', a pre-bonsai that my garden partner, Mo Yee, purchased in a glossy blue pot of Oriental styling. With Mo's blessing, I made the changeover

PLATE 64. A cherry plum (*Prunus cerasifolia*) about 45 years old, on a stack of rocks. Photo by Ken Hollingsworth.

from ceramic to stone, as shown in Plates 62 and 63. Is the *before* better or is the *after* a betterment? Or is one as good as the other? I truly asked the questions without trying to coach the answers. If one or the other looks better to you, then it *is* the better of the two. Mo, anyway, likes the new look. Furthermore, the *spiritual* transformation in the treelet is profound. Removed from its tiny pot, parted from its bonsai context, planted on a piece of the planet, this little spruce no longer urges itself on the gardener as an awkward pre-bonsai in need of all kinds of fuss, such as the thinning and wiring of branches, or in need of a prolonged passage of time—the years it would take before the treelet became a tree with bonsai character. Having renounced any pretense of becoming a bonsai, the treelet immediately becomes a tree comfortable and complete, a citizen of the world rather than of any particular region to my eyes anyway.

I've almost talked myself out of continuing my near-half-century-long pursuit of the art of bonsai, and altogether into growing untrained trees kept small on rocks, or in plain pots, or even on an accommodating railing.

Plate 64 captures a cherry plum (*Prunus cerasifolia*) about 45 years old, on a stack of rocks. *Veronica filiformis,* a useful weed, forms a ground cover about the base of the plum tree. About the base of the stacked rocks grows *Epimedium versicolor* 'Sulphureum' still carrying in late March the previous year's winter-reddened leaves.

Treelets Ever, Bonsai Never. Conifers (*Platycladus orientalis* 'Aurea') in my tropical highland garden (Plate 65), grouped on a pebbled concrete railing with stones for companionship and with moss to hold soil about their roots, are all of 4 years old from cuttings but are not really of a dwarf variety. Nor could these treelets ever be bonsai, for the reason that they are unsuited to bonsai training: Their fan-form leaves and branchlets would fight against any rearrangement—and win. My plan for them is just to let them grow taller and then to hold them there, by pruning, at whatever height seems ideal in the setting. This plant, not incidentally, is remarkable in being one of the few ornamentals that will prosper in nearly all garden climates, from the tropics to Saskatoon.

Spruce Train. Spruce trees (*Picea blehnii*) stand here (in Plate 66) in a long line, as clonal as railcars, but on a wall cap whose measure across, 7⅝ inches (19 cm), is exactly the length of standard red bricks—here set crosswise like railroad ties. I would have preferred for this planting a brick railway a couple of inches wider, yet the spruces carry on in perfect health and at a slow rate of growth suited to their place. Eighteen years old when photographed, these spruces had attained an average height of 15 inches (37 cm). This tree species is not naturally dwarf but has here been dramatically restrained by a minimal allotment of soil. With pruning in years to come the planting can be kept at a suitable size almost indefinitely.

These spruces require watering daily or nearly so during spring, summer, and autumn—watering to be skipped of course during rainy weather—and

PLATE 65. Treelets growing on a concrete railing, no pot needed or wanted.

they are given fertilizer in liquid form about every 2 weeks throughout the growing season. Watering in winter is as needed to keep their soil moist. *Picea blehnii* has proved to be reliably root-hardy in this raised frost-prone position within hardiness zone 5. Judging from this planting, the species is one of the more shade-tolerant conifers. The spruces receive little more than an hour's direct sunshine on a summer day, all that is admitted by oak and dogwood canopies overhead.

A garden friend of ours, Robert Hearst, grew the spruce trees from seed and gave part of the batch of well-grown youngsters to my brother Ken and me. The wall on which we display them stands beside the front door steps of Ken and Phyllis's house, and is integral to its design: The line of living spruce added to the wall becomes part of the architecture and would be grotesque if it failed to fit in, but it does. Granted, the elevated trees bring on the usual platform garden response of stunned surprise at first sight (I speak for myself as much as for anyone else), but after that one's mental computer goes to work noting the color, form, texture, and ecological persuasion of the trees and their moss ground cover (*Homalothecium*) vis-à-vis the building's tan clapboard, brick-work, and vaguely F. L. Wrightian prairie house patrimony, plus the woodland community

PLATE 66. Spruce train (*Picea blehnii*) on a brick rail.

in which the house is tucked away. And it all comes together as winningly as three plums. I'm not sure though that the building's architect would agree: Artists naturally dislike having their work embellished by others. But I'm pleased to report (more honestly, I'm gloating when I say) that a number of visitors have been boggled and delighted on discovering this planting.

Afterword. In the late summer of 2002 a horde of city squirrels, attracted by a bumper crop of acorns in the oak trees that shade the spruces on the railing, invaded. They roughed up the spruce planting, singling it out I suppose as an easily remembered place in which to bury their acorn loot. Repairing their damages, replacing soil and tattered moss as best as could be done, was of no use. The squirrels kept coming back for more tearing and burying.

I call them city squirrels because they have long made a specialty of urban life close to people who shed scraps of edible garbage in parks and wayside places, and other people who purposely feed them. In recent years the squirrels, now too numerous for easy pickings in town, have pushed out into suburbs and even into surrounding woodlands. These aggressive animals might be tolerable if they belonged here in the first place as natives, but the fact is they've migrated from America's eastern cities to the Pacific Northwest, or have been brought here as pets. By now they have driven our charming native chipmunk to extinction in most of its suburban habitats and have chased the shy Douglas squirrel, indigenous to our woods, from much of its range.

Gardeners deal with unwanted squirrels in various ways. A decisive weapon against them is poison grain (manufactured as a remedy for rats) put out where they will find it—probably an illegal measure but not uncommon. In kindly contrast is the trapping of squirrels in baited box traps, followed by the transporting of the temporary captives to some place far away. Bribing the squirrels to leave your garden alone is another crafty method of control, a ploy used for many years by the late Mrs. A. O. U. Berry of the Berry Botanical Gardens in Portland, Oregon. I well remember seeing a stack of big sacks of Quaker brand oats sheltered there outside her house, squirrel feed for some time to come. Mrs. Berry bought them off (so she informed me) by providing them with rolled oats, a food too crumbly and perishable for them to bury, and in quantity sufficient to turn their interest from tearing up the garden in search for other food. I didn't ask about the effectiveness of the scheme.

Less than effective in controlling squirrels but cathartic of pent-up squirrel rage were the actions of the late Carl S. English Jr., a Seattle-based horticulturist and home gardener. I stopped by his garden one day when his wife, Edith, a zoologist and devoted squirrel feeder, was away on some errand. Carl was usually a mild soft-spoken man, but at this moment he'd gone berserk over city squirrels, marauders in his alpine house, despoilers of rarities in his garden of miniature shade plants. He ran after his enemies hurling pot after pot of red terra-cotta. The smashing of crockery underscored the chaos of his cussing, but he never quite scored a hit; the squirrels were too adroit at dodging.

Some of our states have an open season on squirrels where they are hunted as a delicacy. I gather from the writing of squirrel specialist Robert E. Kenwar DPhil in an encyclopedia of mammals that dining on squirrels should be encouraged, particularly in areas where they strip trees of bark as they will do when they lack other food in winter: "There is often no alternative to killing squirrels, so perhaps future research should concentrate on how best to prepare squirrel pie."

If you are not that hungry, try the netting method: It is the cleanest and quickest of anti-squirrel maneuvers for use legally in the home garden. I've used it in several properties. Ken and Phyllis are using it to keep the squirrels off the railing garden of spruces. They bought a bundle of crop netting, the kind made as a cover for ripening berries and other fruits to thwart rapacious birds, and have protected the railing garden with it by cutting slits in the netting, poking the spruce trees—tops, boughs, and trunks—through the slits, and then fitting the netting neatly about the base of the trees. Appearance? Not bad at all, with the netting hardly visible at a little distance. Effectiveness? Almost total. The determined squirrels have tested the barrier, with minor damage resulting, but then have gone elsewhere with their acorns.

Bromeliads on a Slab of Lava. During my lifetime of gardening, a time in which I've grown about four thousand kinds of plants ranging from trees to mosses and from xerophytes to aquatics,

PLATE 67. The edge of a concrete pad is partly covered with a rockery, including this rock-top planting of bromeliads.

in gardens located in tropical, subtropical, and temperate climates, I have come to feel that I understand plant life and its needs reasonably well. But I may never understand the aerial species of bromeliads. There are the neoregelias which, in Nature, perch on tree branches in a little humus, and from that, and from a soup of rain water and decaying organic matter caught in cups at the bases of their leaves, draw enough sustenance to construct a bushel- or bear-size mass of foliage. There are the lesser *Tillandsia* species, clingers on tree bark and stones by a few ridiculously skimpy roots, apparently nothing more than holdfasts without food-gathering function. Yet, the plants gather all they need to build their bodies—from what? Science has worked out some answers and may be perfectly satisfied that there is nothing inexplicable about bromeliads, but I'm not.

The three kinds of bromeliads growing on a slab of lava rock in our New Zealand garden (Plate 67) have all increased into clumps from small starts of a rosette or two placed here 6 years earlier. Uppermost on the stone is a *Neoregelia* hybrid, one of dozens or, more likely, hundreds of horticultural hybrids in the genus: Fanciers have been busy. When planted, in a shallow concavity in the stone, the *Neoregelia* received its lifetime allotment of soil: about 2 cupfuls of a gritty mix. The curly-leaved *Tillandsia butzii* (to the left of the *Neoregelia*) received no soil, nor wanted any. The plant is anchored in place by stones about the size of bricks wedged against its bulbous base. The third bromeliad, the gray-rosetted *T. bergeri*, is similarly held on the rock by smaller stones.

The three have been joined on their perch by a silvery lichen, *Parmelia conspersa*, that has come on its own and grown to about 5 inches (13 cm) across in the same span of years. The ways of the lichen, I can understand. Its life plan is to lie low on the rock, emulating its host in being hard, dry, and mineral-like, while slowly dissolving and absorbing minute amounts of mineral that are quite enough for a lichen's subsistence. But the relatively gigantic growth of the bromeliads on so little food surpasses my understanding.

With the tillandsias there is another puzzle: While the neoregelias pay for their garden upkeep with rich colors and big leafage of landscape value, why do I and thousands of other gardeners grow the lesser tillandsias—these quiet spiders of leafage whose little flowers offer only a flicker of color? Well, there are showy exceptions such as *Tillandsia cyanea*. But let the question stand. I have no answer other than a suspicion that we *Tillandsia* buffs grow these uncanny plants simply because they have us—in the words of an old tune—bewitched, bothered, and bewildered.

On Pavement, Railing, Rock-top, or Pier? The planting in Plate 68 may lay claim to occupying any or all of the aforementioned places, but I think of it as a garden on a railing. Technically, the 28-foot- (8.5-m-) long structure that supports the garden is a pier whose cemented granite rocks keep a mountain brook—one that rises and roars during hard rain—from cascading down the sixty steps that lead upward to my museum of tribal sculpture here at Banaue village in the rice terrace country of the northern Philippines. Along the

pier/railing/collective rock top, I (with help) have arranged boulders, the largest weighing about 600 pounds (300 kg).

In between these boulders, in a soil depth of 1 to 9 inches (2.5 to 23 cm), I grow plants I've counted on being drought-tolerant, and they have all obliged. Among them are bromeliads of the genus *Dyckia*; *Agave*; *Sedum dasyphyllum*; several recently developed, small-growing forms of crown of thorns (*Euphorbia milii*) with rosy, pink, or yellow flowers; and a miniature wandering Jew (*Callisia repens*), planted in only an inch (2.5 cm) depth of soil and separated from other plantings, by bare patches of pavement, to control its invasiveness. (Some of these plants are not present in the photo which was taken a year or so before they were planted.)

But those rocks: It took the muscle power of six strong men to shoulder them up the sixty steps and onto the railing. For the carry, the men rigged a litter out of two poles (tree trunks about as thick as a person's thigh) with a sling of wire mesh nailed to the wood. One at a time the stones were rolled onto the sling, stone and poles hoisted onto shoulders, and tussled up the steps to the top of the railing. At its far end, where the largest of the stones were lifted off the litter and into place, is a 50-foot (15.3-m) drop into a gorge which the brook, over millennia, has carved into solid stone. The men—rice farmers when not doing odd jobs such as this—were barefoot, as they are accustomed to being while working their terraces, the better to brace themselves on stone walls and in the mud of the rice fields. Today, the men performed perhaps

PLATE 68. Drought-tolerant plants on a railing of mortared stones.

the oddest of jobs ever in their careers. Shouldering poles and stone, they lurched along the narrow railing, swaying with the swinging of the massive stone in its sling, bare feet at times halfway on the pavement, halfway off its edge and in space. The danger of it all scared the begeebers out of me, as I, from my place of firm footing on the steps, stood directing the positioning of the rocks. "That's good enough," I remember calling out. "Come on back. I wouldn't want to have to bring up your children." But the men seemed unconcerned, and after the job was finished we all joshed and guzzled a beer apiece, cold from the museum's refrigerator, on a hot day unusual in these mountains.

Cliff Ferns. Plate 69 frames three giant ferns of shuttlecock form, three of a dozen nest ferns (*Asplenium nidus*), in sizes up to 6 feet (1.8 m) wide, planted on a cliff of silt-stone in my tropical highland garden. For the landscaper, this fern species and other nest ferns of almost identical size and form are among the most valuable tropical plants. With their outwardly thrusting broad-blade leaves, they make a kind of green explosion up to 12 feet (3.7 m) across, in time. A few of these will fill a lot of empty space with powerful foliage, yet they blend easily with other plants larger or smaller than themselves. Nest ferns are epiphytes in the wild but adapt readily to a terrestrial life in fast-draining soil.

To grow them on a cliff, we constructed hemispherical baskets—on the lines of the nests of cliff swallows or swifts—to hold their roots. Where the

PLATE 69. Nest ferns (*Asplenium nidus*) affixed to a cliff.

birds use self-made glue to fix their nests on cliff faces, we used concrete nails: two nails driven into crevices in the stone, about 18 inches (46 cm) apart, on either side of the spot where we wanted to center a fern; and a third nail hammered in about 18 inches below the others and midway between them. To the upper two nails, we attached a half-hoop of number ten galvanized wire. And then, with rattan split to the thickness of rawhide shoelaces and attached to the wire hoop and to the lowermost nail, we wove for each fern a bracket-form basket, using a fish-net stitching with sizable 2- to 3-inch (5- to 7.5-cm) spaces between the stitches (the netting might have caught salmon but not trout). Before I go any further I should, in honesty, catch myself up for claiming that "we" did all this. It was the handiwork of my wonderfully able assistant, Egoy, with me standing around. My right-hand man then lined each basket with a native woodland moss instead of sphagnum, eased the root mass of each fern into its basket, and packed in soil enough to fill the basket to the brim. Egoy, by the way, together with his wife, Fe, and their children, manage my museum in the mountains and maintain the garden there, of which the fern planting is a part.

Several years have passed since he and I nestled the nest ferns on the cliff. The rattan, having become brittle with age, has broken in places, but the ferns have become even more firmly affixed to the stone than at first. Their support wires (hidden by moss and by root growth) remain uncorroded and on the job, while their roots—a felt-like wad of almost microscopically fine division—hold the soil in place and adhere to the cliff face as stubbornly as the webbing of a mussel on a tidal boulder.

This same bracket basket technique can be used to grow many other kinds of plants on fences or on walls of concrete or brick, as well as on cliffs. I've used a smaller 7-inch- (18-cm-) wide version of the basket to grow African violets and Christmas cactus on a shaded fence. In place of the relatively short-lived rattan that we have used as netting material, I would recommend a heavy-duty nylon fish line, which will be longer-lasting by years and can be mostly concealed at the start by tucking around it some of the moss or fiber used to line the basket.

Planted Ruin. Plants have a way of alighting as seed on any mellowing and ruining stone architecture, and prospering there on what seems

PLATE 70. A planted "ruin," or call it a garden folly.

impossibly little nourishment. If left alone for long these plants will make hanging gardens of the most monumental stonework such as that of the Mayans, the Cambodians, and the Romans. The Coliseum in Rome, before being cleared of its clinging plants centuries ago, had become a cliffy woods, home to hundreds of kinds of trees, shrubs, and perennials. And in our own time, garden walls and pasture walls of stone attract their own adventurous kinds of greenery, which proclaim the territory as rightfully theirs and ourselves as a mere short-term impediment.

With an appreciation of all this as a motive, I set up my own leafy ruin in the mid-1990s (Plate 70). The location is on Samar Island in the Philippines, on the property of garden friends of mine, the Ida family. Despite the Asian location, the evocation of my ruin with plants is in certain prehistoric Polynesian monuments, brutally plain stacks of rough coral rocks.

The eastern part of Samar Island where I garden is a boney land of outcropping limestone, the remains of ancient coral reefs. The stone is a constant challenge to local farm families, who make up most of the population. They gain arable ground only by breaking the stone with sledge-hammers and clearing it away with pry bars. The main crops are coconuts and sweet potatoes; the growing of rice, the preferred staple, is impossible here. Farm families who work the stoniest ground make a little money by selling stone for use in construction. Limestone fragments the size of piglets and porkers are hammered free from the outcrops and stacked beside roadways in neatly squared ricks 3 feet (90 cm) high and wide, and as many feet long as the stone harvesters have stones to stack. Sales are infrequent. The rick of stones waits beside the road for months. When a buyer finally materializes, the event may be celebrated at the seller's dinner table.

On two occasions a year apart, I bought stones for making a planted ruin and another project. I handed money for the stones to farm wives, whose husbands and sons were some distance away, out of sight and beyond calling, tending to their plant-ings. Both women concluded the transactions with exactly the same words, spoken in the same tone of quiet dignity and rightfulness, "Now I can buy rice."

Two flatbed truckloads of stones heaped high went into the making of my simulated ruin—a simulation of what? A pagan altar perhaps. At any rate a thing that is less than a temple and more than a dog's grave, 14 feet (4.3 m) long, 5½ feet (1.7 m) high, with two stone wings not visible in the color plate. Without Christian intent, the design turned out to be cruciform. This structure of rough, unmortared rocks is full of sizable inter-spaces. I've filled some of the voids with bushel after bushel of stone chips, hand-hammered to about the size of broken hazelnut shells, a second-ary product of the stone-sellers.

When planting the ruin I scooped pockets in the stone chips, set a plant in each pocket, and filled in about its roots with a few trowelfuls of composty soil—soil in plenty for bromeliads including the pineapple of agriculture, which is usually a terrestrial but is an able perching plant as well. Other epiphytes and petrophytes at home on the ruin include—and here I have a purpose in piling up a lot of plant names and place names—

the succulents *Kalanchoe pinnata,* a Madagascar native ocean-transported and naturalized on Samar Island's seaside limestone; *K. integra,* Central African, a plant with glaucous leaves and yellow flowers; *Rhoeo spathacea,* originally tropical American, now a pan-tropical well-known as Moses-in-the-boat; and *Pilea nummularifolia,* South American. This last-named species, with its rounded, rugose leaves on trailing stems, is an easy house plant anywhere, and is in the tropics a vigorous ground cover and sprawler over moist rocks without any soil at all, once you start it in a soil pocket as I've done here.

The planted ruin rests on a platform of dressed stone pavers in an open area surrounded by planted riches of tropical foliages and flowers: *Hymenocallis littoralis,* South American, in white flower at lower left in the color plate; *Ensete ventricosum,* Abyssinian banana; *Polyscias fruticosa,*

PLATE 71. *Sleeping Grouse,* a 1962 sculpture by James Washington Jr. The bird dozes in a nest of the moss *Racomitrum lanuginosum,* the same species growing on the granite dome in Plate 58.

ming aralia, native to India and Polynesia; *Bambusa glaucescens,* a bamboo of Indo-Chinese origin; and several others. All of these plants and several of those on the rocks of the ruin came to me as divisions purchased from villagers with tiny front gardens, in Guiuan (rhymes with key-wan), a fishing port 6 miles (10 km) away. By what means and devious routing each of these plants had arrived in this remote outpost of civilization, from one and another far-flung landfalls, is a separate unrecorded episode in the annals of pleasure gardening, unreasonable calling that it is. No matter that these plants can't be eaten or utilized in any practical way. They are a spirit tonic whose value must rank not far behind bodily sustenance by rice or wheat.

Afterword. About 2 years following the installation of the planted ruin, an unseen, unknown, uninvited, but not unwelcome visitor arrived at the ruin, his curiosity alerted by a paved pathway that leads from a public road to the stonework. I'm assuming that it was a man, because his response to what he encountered would be quite out of character with any woman or child in the local population. At some time he revisited the ruin and brought with him two containers of paint, and a paint brush, evidently a narrow one. On one of the pavers at the base of the ruin he painted the name

ROQUE in block letters of yellow, lined on one side of each letter with brown, in a careful job befitting a statement of faith. The painter had seen and interpreted my planted ruin as an altar, and had dedicated it to San Roque, whose name translates as Saint Rock or Saint of the Rocks. The legend of this sanctified Frenchman came by way of Italy and Spain to the Philippines, and here San Roque has become one of the people's several favorite *santos,* selected from a heavenly community of saints numbering some three thousand. His coming is a mystery of migration and adoration blended in my mind with that of Guiuan's garden plants.

Planted Sculpture. Atop a rock, atop a railing, a granite bird dozes in a nest of moss (Plate 71). I hesitate before telling you—thereby dispelling the usual fiction in published garden pictures, that what we see is on its own, self-perfected, with no care or worry or destructive force at work in the world in view—but the truth is, I usually keep the stone bird and the moss covered with fine nylon netting, which I removed before taking the picture. The moss is a particularly fluffy and cozy kind, ideal as nesting material. The jays and robins won't leave it alone. The present batch of moss is not the first I've grown here.

CHAPTER SIX

On Stumps and Logs

PLATE 72. A 14-foot-(4.3-m-) wide stump of a western red cedar felled late in the nineteenth century. Hemlock trees (*Tsuga heterophylla*), seeded atop the decaying stump, have plunged their roots down to the soil below. The plant in the foreground is *Polystichum munitum*, one of the several most stalwart, landscape-worthy ferns for Pacific Slope gardens, from northern California to Alaska.

Trees that fall to the forest floor lie there as logs, surrendered and peaceable, but tree stumps and snags do not go gentle; they stand resolutely and register, as they age and erode, deepened messages the like of those in old faces. When incorporated in a garden, a sizable old stump becomes a memorial sculpture of great presence. Nature, or a gardener, may establish plantings atop a stump, turning it into a platform garden, but gardeners more often will place a vine against the shaft of a tree stump, making a planted sculpture of it.

Some other gardeners are so admiring of an appealing stump that they will, with major effort, haul it from someplace else into their gardens. I've done that along with stump gardening of other sorts, but some of the compositions I've put together and think of as stump gardening are actually made with logs or lengths of tree trunk upended, buried at one end, and planted at the other.

The art of stump and log gardening is especially appropriate in any forested or formerly forested region, notably in coastal British Columbia and in the Pacific Northwest of the United States. Here many gardeners have inherited on their properties the massive stumps of conifers logged in the nineteenth or early twentieth centuries. The old-time loggers, standing two together on platforms, cut the trees high up—as much as twice man-height, where the trunk tapered inward enough from its flared base to be felled with a crosscut saw. The stumps they left, now treasured as garden features by discerning property owners, often measure as wide as a person's outstretched arms, or even twice that; they serve as awesome reminders of virgin forest. One looks at these relics and wonders, Did such trees really grow here? The proof still stands, albeit crumblingly. Fifty years more will largely erase these stumps, but that *is* a half century longer.

The old stumps are more than relics of the region's Paul Bunyan years. Many of them are stages where morality plays are in progress, acted out by native plants that have taken root here and thrived, providing capsule demonstrations of the will of greenery to regain the world whenever our day may be done. We see trees, especially hemlocks (*Tsuga heterophylla*), of considerable trunk measure, arising from stump tops, driving their roots down through decaying wood and finally into the ground (Plate 72). We often see atop the conifer stumps shaggy aggregations of plants including, in addition to trees, berry-bearing shrubbery such as salal (*Gaultheria shallon*), elder (*Sambucus racemosa*), and red huckleberry (*Vaccinium parvifolium*), seeded there by birds. And at the bases of these stump-top trees and shrubs grow toadstools, lichens, mosses, and ferns, which came as spores carried by breezes. Altogether, the plant community reprises, in little, the three-tiered makeup of an entire forest: canopy, undergrowth, and groundlings. The region is one of only several places on earth, outside the tropics, where this natural forestation of stumps takes place.

When the stumps were younger, early in the post-logging era, they were by no means considered noble and artistic as they are now. They were more the depressing symbols of a boom time that had rushed by, leaving stump-stubbled acreages from which farm families now wrested a living. During the 1930s when I was a boy in Bothell, then a ranch and farm town near Seattle, we townies used the term "stump farmers" when referring, with neither prejudice nor sympathy, to those families, some of them migrants from the Dust Bowl, who had settled on the thin, leached soil of logged-off hillsides outside town, beyond the more availing valley land where earlier settlers had homesteaded. Then, during the post–Second World War years, the stump farms were divided into lots for housing and those conifer stumps that remained came to be viewed nostalgically.

Stump and Log Garden Tours

Although tree stumps are often gardened by being covered with plants until they are lost to sight, or are occasionally, by means of creative pruning, left partially exposed as garden sculpture, other possibilities exist, rich adventures to be realized in gardening these monuments of fallen trees. Logs, too, can live again by placing gardens on them. Examples follow.

Stump with Bird Gifts. In Plate 73 a conifer stump felled at the turn of the twentieth century teems with a decade's old, bird-brought planting of salal and red huckleberry (the taller of the shrubs). The stump stands in a Pacific Northwest garden. Kurume azaleas grow near its base, and on its 11-foot- (3.4-m-) tall shaft grows the clinging vine *Hydrangea anomala* (zone 4). After another year or two of free growth, which will encourage the formation of its platter-form clusters of white flowers, the vine will need a rigorous annual pruning to keep it from muffling the stump with leafage.

With control, this *Hydrangea* species is an excellent choice for the gardening of a tall stump; the vine's leaves have the size, and its branches the range, to begreen a broad and tall wood surface. English ivy (*Hedera helix*) in its big-leaved, big-growing form is another vine that will require yearly control to keep it from taking over any stump that has sculptural value in itself.

If, however, your aim is to have the stump disappear beneath vine growth, a large number of vine species are all too willing to perform that service and then go on to take over a goodly part of any home lot. A smaller number of vines are quite busy enough about themselves to cover a stump completely within several years yet are not so hyperactive as to be practically uncontrollable. They *will* need pruning but usually not in haystack amounts. The names of some of these vines are *Ampelopsis brevipendunculata*, colorful of leaf in its form, *A. brevipendunculata* 'Elegans', hardy down to zone 6; *Hedera colchica*, Persian ivy, zone 6; *Hedera helix*, zone 5, in quite a few of its many juvenile forms; *Jasminum officinale*, true jasmine, zone 7; *Lonicera heckrottii*, goldflame honeysuckle, with showy, richly fragrant flowers, zone 5; *Muehlenbeckia complexa*, mattress vine, zone 7; *Parthenocissus quinquefolia*, Virginia creeper, zone 3; and *Trachelospermum jasminoides*, star jasmine, zone 8. Except for the Virginia creeper, a clinging vine, the rest of these will need to be fixed to the stump in their first year to get them started up its side.

Viney clematis species bring a flocculent display of flowers to the stump garden and are somewhat more controllable than the vines in the list above. Clematis are more the stump companions in that they will let their stump retain a peekaboo presence. Some pruning will still be needed for any balance of leaf and of monument. Any of the viney clematis will make good stump companions, except for one. Eschew for this use, and any other garden use except perhaps the festooning of some killer cliff, the overpowering *Clematis armandii*. I don't know how many gardeners—several anyway—that I've heard lamenting their mistake, or that of their landscaper, in having planted this thuggish vine. It is stronger in its will to expand than is the will to prune in most gardeners.

Less combative as a vine cover for stumps is *Clematis montana*, both the species and its several hybrids. These make vigorous growth, to be pruned soon after the spectacular spring flowering of the vine, which comes on old wood. Lesser still in their branch growth are *C. macropetala,* which I've found easy to grow from seed, and *C. alpina*. My garden friend Margaret Mulligan and I set out a mail-order plant of the latter species at the base of a large stump in her garden. The vine needed support with small nails and loops of string to fix it on the wood during its first two summers (the *Hydrangea* and the ivy usually need no such help), but once the *Clematis* got going it turned itself into a quite delightful lace of foliage and softly violet flowers against the wood.

All the aforenamed clematis are hardy in about zone 4 or in an even colder climate. Gardeners in subtropical and tropical regions may grow, as stump covering, such vines as *Allamanda neriifolia* or *Aristolochia gigantea*. Flowers of the latter-named vine are huge, purplish and mottled, and fascinatingly ugly, like a floral contraption made of sliced liver.

Stump Sculpture. Plate 74 shows a stump with no platform at top, hence no place in platform gardening, but with magnificent stance as a garden sculpture. The stump (or snag) is that of a western red cedar (*Thuja plicata*), left standing during logging operations early in the twentieth century. In 1969 this stump was excavated in sections, loaded

PLATE 74. A 30-foot- (9.1-m-) tall stump of western red cedar trucked to a public garden and set up as a sculpture.

onto a flatbed truck, and transported to the Park and Tilford Garden in North Vancouver. There landscaper Harry Webb had his crew char the surfaces of the stump with a blowtorch, especially those of the stump's hollow interior, to deter the decay of the wood, a preservation technique learned from native Canadians who, during centuries of their tribal life hereabout, charred the surfaces of the cedar planks they split and used in their

PLATE 73. A century-old stump capped with fruit-bearing shrubbery planted by birds.

buildings. Webb's crew partly buried the stump for stability, which was further ensured by a star-shaped steel brace bolted to the inside of the stump's sections to hold them together. That much done, the crew planted a young tree beside the forest relic; with fine appropriateness it is a western red cedar. In the color plate, you see it 31 years later, outstripping the stump. The crew also planted, at the stump's base, English ivy in its big-leaved form. The ivy climbed the wood at the rate of a foot (30 cm) or better each year; 30 years on, Park and Tilford gardeners cut the vine well back, as you see it, thereby bringing much of the stump surface back into view.

Stump Duo. Small stumps make an effective garden feature in a small area. The two pieces of wood in Plate 75 are not exactly stumps but unsplit fireplace logs, employed as a stumpery. I've dug them into the ground a little, here beside a path, leaving 2 feet (60 cm) of wood above ground, and have planted the tops of each with moss (*Brachythecium*), pressed onto a scant sprinkling of soil. By some small miracle, active during the three springtimes since, no robin has yet carried off the moss for its nest.

Porch Size. Another small-scale stump garden composition is the ensemble in Plate 76 on our front porch in Auckland, sheltered by the deep eaves of the house. To hold the stump (actually a Kauri wood log) upright, I planted it in a soil-filled tub; about its base grow juvenile forms of English ivy (*Hedera helix* 'Carolina Crinkle' and *H. helix* 'Lutzii'—the one with marbled, softly yellow, softly

green leaves). In the illustration, we see these 8 years later. The ivies have grown over the wooden tub, completely hiding it, for which I'm grateful. They require yearly pruning, which I don't mind doing, to keep them from engulfing the stump and growing over a planting of succulents in a slight hollow at its top. The largest of these inhabitants of the stump top is the entertaining *Haworthia turgida*, with its jolly fat (turgid) leaves, soapstone green in color except for translucent patches which form a pattern that suggests an abstract stained glass window.

In the background is the shrub-like succulent *Crassula tetragona*, here a decade old, 2½ feet (75 cm) tall. This species is one of the most staid of the smaller succulents, a group of garden plants more often notable for their tendency not to stay but to die out in their older portions. *Crassula tetragona* is also one of the world's gold medal Olympian survivors of neglect. As a container plant it will come through months with no rain or irrigation, no fertilizer or grooming, and yet stay healthy and tidy, as may be seen in the picture. I would not purposely be that crass with the *Crassula*, but I know that it happens here during my months of absence. In its remote position at the back of the stump, the plant is not watered or attended to in any way.

Other Olympians in this stump-and-tub garden, gold medallists in the drought trials and the all-around neglect marathon, are the Brazilian bromeliad *Aechmea* 'Red Wine', with its glossy strap leaves (at left in the color plate); and the

PLATE 75. Two small stumps placed beside a garden path and planted with moss.

South African succulent plant, *Haworthia fasciata*, a colony of harmlessly spiky olive-green, gray-banded leaves in rosettes—about twenty such rosettes in this two-decade-old plant. The species is a slow-grower, and like the *Crassula*, a determined stayer.

Stump Garden Shocker. At the entrance to my museum of tribal sculpture in the mountains of northern Luzon, I've stationed this large tree stump capped with a stone sacred to the Ifugao people of this region (Plate 77). It is a completely natural and uncarved volcanic rock whose phallic form closely repeats in small scale that of the great Cro-Magnon menhir at Champ-Dolent in France. The Ifugao monument stood for centuries propped up in a rice field, where it bolstered the fertility of the annual crop. I purchased the stone from a pagan rice farmer who had inherited it along with the field in which it stood. Lately, the farmer's Christianized son and heir had announced his plans to break the stone in two, to make a handy pair of firedogs out of it. The father decided that such an iconoclastic act would stir up wrath in the spirit world—better to sell.

So now this artifact stands atop a tree stump that has been carved a little at its apex, cupped to receive and support the stone relic. A planting of ferns (*Nephrolepis cordifolia*, in a smallish Asian form), on pavement at the base of the stump, has climbed the wood to just about the ideal height and fullness of growth. I've begun a regimen of yearly pruning (pulling it away) to keep the plant

PLATE 76. Stump staging for an especially interesting plant (at top).

from covering both stump and stone. And on the museum's wall close by I've posted a sign that honors the local Animist belief in the stone's powers as a fertility agent, and cautions that to embrace the icon, as museum visitors are apt to do while somebody in their group snaps a picture, is to bring on, in pagan assurance, pregnancy.

Certain other visitors are put off by the graphic symbolism in this stone. A clergyman who was touring the garden with a group of

PLATE 77. A stump holds a stone sacred to pagan Ifugao people.

Canadian students, average age about twenty, became apoplectic with outrage at the sight of it. "All right, kids, let's go," he demanded, and rounding up his flock, he leddeth them from temptation. But for most visitors the standing stone is apparently received as innocuous, or not seen as phallic at all. A carpenter who worked on the museum's interior used to spend his lunch hours seated on an arm of the tree stump. He likened the stump-and-stone to a volcano and nothing more.

Log Supine. Brought home from a woodland and resettled beside a shaded walkway, the nurse log in Plate 78 carries on nurturing. The plants in its care include mosses, a colony of licorice ferns (*Polypodium glycyrrhiza*), and a lone deer fern (*Blechnum spicant*). The term "nurse log," if unfamiliar, is applied respectfully to decaying logs that provide both surface and substance for the growth of native plant seedlings, and so play a major role in renewing the forest. Nurse logs are, of course, to

PLATE 78. Nurse log salvaged and brought to a home garden from a forest soon to be logged.

be left alone where found in a woodland preserve, but where woods are to be cut, any decaying log salvageable by a gardener is for the taking with a clear conscience. Gardener Gilbert Eades saved the nurse log we see, trucked it home from privately owned forest acreage in the foothills of the Cascade Mountains, land scheduled to be razed in preparation for "development." Mr. Eades also salvaged a sizable snag and has set it up in the manner of the Park and Tilford snag sculpture, as a sentinel at his garden's entrance. He has as well brought home truckloads of moss (*Drepanocladus*) with which he has carpeted thousands of square feet of shaded ground in his garden.

Logs Upright. Plate 79 exhibits an informal columnade or postade of logs in our Auckland garden; the grouping has five logs but only three are in view. The above-ground portions of the logs, whose lower ends are buried supportively in the ground, vary from 3 to 5 feet (90 to 120 cm) in height. On top of each log is a cap of plants growing in a little composty soil. Among them are the cactus *Rhipsalis tucumanensis* and several bromeliads including *Nidularium regelioides*, rosy at the center of its green leaf rosettes; a red-leaved *Neoregelia* hybrid; and an *Aechmea* bearing stems of apricot-orange-colored berries. The huge, slashed, shield-form foliage in the background belongs to *Monstera deliciosa*. The bromeliads, epiphytes in Nature, remind me of another South American tree dweller, the sloth, as creatures of protracted mental and physical processes; the broms are, of

PLATE 79. Logs set up as posts and planted at top with bromeliads.

course, slower by far than even the sloth, nearly changeless for months on end, yet always freshly green, and in season flower- and berry-bearing. You can count on a repeat performance year after year.

Bromeliads of the genera I've named have the leaf size and mass, and the patience, to be among the most rewarding plants for platform gardening. Late in his career the renowned Brazilian garden architect Roberto Burle Marx designed for the growing of these plants, native to his home country, a tall scaffolding which was in part platform garden and in part a highly stylized tree sculpture, with foliage formed by the bushel-size leaf bunches of the bromeliads fixed high up on the structure.

My own platform garden of bromeliads grows on tree fern logs, which will last up to a half century without decaying. The bromeliads on this "postade" have received almost no care and have needed almost none, since I planted them here several years before taking the picture you see. When I'm away, for many months, these plants are on their own. When I'm here I give them an annual grooming by pulling or cutting away a few spent leaves and with my fingers I rake off the somewhat unsightly webbing spun by spiders—tunneled lairs of spider silk leading deeply in among the bromeliad leaves. The spiders sleep within by day but come out at night and restore their web tunnels totally by the morning after I've removed them. Mine is an exercise of futility and theirs is one of a webbed tenacity stretching back to Paleozoic time. Since they are invaluable hunters of roving insects that feed on garden plants other than the bromeliads (eaten by nothing anywhere I've grown them), these spiders are not to be destroyed. They are the actual custodians of the platform garden, and I am no more than a momentary vandal in their midst.

On that topic—the vandalism of a natural community—by what planetary permission do I make use of the trunks of tree ferns, as I do here and also in the Philippines, that have been cut down for sale to gardeners and carvers? By permission I believe to be considerable but by no means categorical. Tree ferns seed themselves as first-comers on cut-over forest land. They form a constantly self-renewing resource. The hillsides on which they grow, and from which they are taken, would seem, in a shallow reckoning at least, to lose only the humus that would come of their fallen fronds and trunks.

Stumps Upside Down. Large tree stumps, dug from the ground with machinery or with pick and shovel, and turned upside down—roots skyward and trunk earthward (Plates 80 and 81)—present not only an altered appearance, but also gardening prospects distinct from those of stumps rightside up. In appearance, many inverted stumps are crudely anatomical. Some suggest a human hand complete with a wrist (the underground part of the tree trunk), a palm (the rough platter formed by the confluence of the stump's main roots), and fingers (extending roots). Hand-like stumps are easily prepared for platform gardening by plugging any holes in the palm and then covering the palmate surface with an airy soil mix 6–8 inches (15–20 cm)

PLATE 80. An upside-down stump exhibiting the holeyness of a Henry Moore; the planting consists of ferns and *dongla*, a red-leaved form of *Cordyline terminalis*, almost certainly one of the world's oldest cultivated varieties of a plant species.

deep. Any turned-over stump that is highly irregular and perhaps not at all hand-like may make an attractive display on its own as sculpture. In fact there are certain excavated stumps that display the inventiveness of a Henry Moore bronze, with quite as many anthropomorphic swoops, knobs, holes, and hollows. For some of us the wooden counterpart is entirely as satisfactory as the metal imitation and is available for a tiny fraction of the price. The stump as sculpture really needs no embellishment with plants grown directly on the wood but may be made the better—the more easeful in the garden— with a planting at its base.

The inverted stumps I have to show you are hand-shaped and planted mainly with ferns, shrubbery, and perennials native to the stumps' locale, Ifugao Province, mile- (1.6-km-) high in the Philippine Cordillera. The red-leaved shrub in Plate 80 is *Cordyline terminalis*, in a clonal selection the Ifugao people call *dongla*. The plant is sacred in their tribal belief. They grow it on the narrow footpaths at the top of their rice terrace walls, where they believe it protects the crop and the growers. They wear its leaves in their hair during ceremonial dances that pacify the spirits of warriors slain by their ancestors. Powerful magic, the *dongla* shrub. I feel sure that Ifugao brought it with them when they migrated here from southern China several thousand years ago. How sure? I see the shrub in historic photographs taken by the U.S. Army during its administration here following the Spanish-American War of 1898. The Americans didn't bring the *dongla* nor did the Spaniards who preceded them: they weren't here as horticulturists. *Dongla*, with its presumed ancient origin with the Ifugao, must be one of the world's oldest cultivated varieties of an ornamental plant.

In the stump garden where the *dongla* grows, I've placed a reflection pool in the form of a wooden bowl filled with water. Three others of my five stump gardens in this location hold similar bowls. They are reclaimed farmyard feeders carved from naturally hemispherical burls found on old pine trees (*Pinus kesiya*) native to the regional mountains. These wens of pine trees are so saturated with congealed pitch that the wood seems halfway amberized. Bowls made from the burls are remarkably resistant to decay. Two of the burl bowls I display as water-mirrors were farm family heirlooms dating back to the nineteenth century, and in daily use as poultry or piglet feeders for more than 100 years. I've worked up a reverent sentimentality toward them that is probably equal to that the British feel for their antique stone troughs, now trough gardens.

Five upside-down stump gardens, four in a line at one side of a trail, one at the other side. The trail leads through the property of my garden friends, Noel and Gloria Balenga. Nearly every time I come to Ifugao we exchange plants that are reciprocally new to us, and lately the Balengas have invited me to landscape garden on their land. I'm glad for the invitation since the ground available for gardening outside my museum is already packed with plantings.

The Balengas' mountainside property has been in the family for centuries. The steep land is theirs, but the trail leading through it and past their front door is an ancient thoroughfare: Foot-rights endure as a part of common law and community courtesy.

Several times daily, neighbors well known, or villagers from afar who are known at least by face, or even the hardier sort of tourists from anywhere in the world (nearby rice terraces are a World Heritage Site) will hike through the Balenga dooryard on their way up or down the mountain.

My stump gardens occupy precious level ground at trailside. On a Saturday morning—market day morning—a grandmotherly-grandfatherly couple, rice farmers from farther up the mountain, came along the trail on their way to market 3 miles (5 km) down. From their costumes, they were identifiable as pagans, the term by which they refer to themselves, in their adherence to the tribal Animist-Ancestorist religion of their people. The wife, barefoot, wore a store-bought blouse and a traditional, homespun, wrap-around skirt with a red-and-black-pattern. The husband, barefoot as well, was store-attired to the extent of a cotton shirt (the day was chilly); below he wore the Ifugao tribesman's classical red G-string, which covered him in front with a strip of fabric but left him mooning the universe. He held a trail staff with a protective idol carved as a finial.

The couple stopped short when they saw my stump gardens. They began chuckling with that particular mirth brought on by confoundedness. We hear the same from people anywhere when they encounter familiar things (in this instance familiar plants, farmyard feeding bowls, and forest detritus) in unheard of, illogical association. Think of the famous Dadaist teacup lined with fur and

you may share, for a moment, something of this couple's sense of shattered logic. But then they stopped chuckling, became thoughtful, and entered into a chatty analysis of their bizarre sighting. This much of what they said was translated for me, for the couple spoke only Ifugao, which I have not learned except for a few crucial words: They decided that, yes, they could accept this irreligious use of *dongla*, since the spirit world would probably not be displeased; and, yes, they could see ornamental value in plants that had always been to them wayside weeds, now that these plants were extricated from wilderness and provided with staging. My words can be no more than an approximation of theirs. Even so, I feel at ease that I've conveyed the substance of their thoughts. They walked on, giving me a polite nod as they passed by, to which I responded with the words, "*Manong, Manang*," respectful greetings with a gender difference in them.

PLATE 81. An upside-down stump garden with ferns and other foresters and the arm action of an octopus.

CHAPTER SEVEN

Table Gardening

"And now, ladies and gentlemen, the
sensational, levitational, larger-than-life art of
table gardening." There may be enough of the
amazing in table gardening to justify such an
introduction in the florid voice of an emcee.
But in quieter terms, table gardening is the
growing of plants directly on a table without
the use of pots or other containers, an art that
provides gardening opportunities virtually
unavailable by any other means.

PLATE 82. Greenhouse
bench garden. A plank-
sided bench supports ferns
in the greenhouse of
Torben Barfod. At left,
Blechnum penna-marina
(poetically named after the
Sea Pen); at right, a dwarf
form of lady fern, *Athyrium
filix-femina* 'Minutissima'.
A ceramic frog keeps an
eye on things.

For instance, there is the scenic tabletop landscape made up of plants of suitable size (not overly large), often in a composition with stones. An artful tabletop landscape invites that same charmed entry into a different and refreshing world that we also find in any garden big enough to walk within and effective enough to offer us transport. Another of the special effects of a successful table

PLATE 83. Alpine house bench garden. Hen-and-chicks (*Sempervivum*) in variety and hardy *Opuntia* cacti grow on a bench within an open-sided alpine house. Water plants emerge from a pool just outside. Gardener Ilga Jansons designed and planted this handsome architectural complex as a part of her home garden.

garden landscape is something of a sense of levitation: The big-little landscape, in being lofted on a platform, appears only lightly moored, a green islet on the point of breaking free and floating ethereally; or an equally buoyant islet of gray plants.

Few other forms of garden art approach table gardening's equipoise of the grand and the miniature. Of these few, penjing and seikei, the Chinese and Japanese arts of miniature landscaping in containers, usually trays made of ceramic or of chiseled stone, may contain as much scenery as that of a table garden several times larger, yet these Asian art forms tend to be hobbled by symbolism and stylization and dinkiness—qualities which, come to think of it, actually may be a part of the rich satisfactions these arts no doubt provide their practitioners. Table garden landscaping is freer in form, with a larger stage that encourages the gardener to realize the less constrained, less predictable landscape in little, but not too little. Other garden relatives of table landscaping are plant compositions placed on greenhouse or alpine house benches (Plates 82 and 83), but in being mounted on a bench, which is usually attached to and surmounted by a building, the planting lacks much of table gardening's semblance of theater in the round, of theater almost floating free.

The virtually levitating landscape is but one type of table garden. "Ladies and gentlemen, there is also the amazing, self-magnifying tabletop bouquet." In the practice of this type of table garden art, the gardener places a closely spaced planting of annuals or of ornamental foliage plants on a table, and afterward waters and fertilizes them unstintingly—with two results. One, if all goes as well as it should, the tabletop planting will burgeon, billow, and even overflow its platform, turning itself into the like of one of those wonderfully homey, over-stuffed bouquets for which there should be a separate category in flower arrangement shows, there among all the tortuous and unnatural acts with flora. Two, a palpable sense of levitation comes into play again, as in table landscaping, yet here in conjunction with a magnifying effect. On a tabletop, well above ground level, the display of flowers or foliages gains a visual value well beyond that which the same number of plants would have in the open ground below. It is an optical illusion with practical benefits: You can achieve a seemingly lavish showing with relatively few annuals (as in Plate 98) or of other plants at relatively little cost, and perhaps in a location where nothing would prosper if planted in the ground.

Selecting a Table

The basis for all table gardening is a table. What kind, then? Find a table that can pass a physical for furniture. No wobbly or decrepit specimen should be trusted as a base for a garden, but apart from that proviso, almost any table built for outdoor use (with the exception of the average glass-topped table) has strength to spare for this job. The gardens I myself have placed on tables of average (patio table) size weigh as much as 350 pounds (175 kg), when composed of stones in addition to soil and plants. Even my smallest opus, on a table a little less in circumference than that of an automobile tire, weighs about 75 pounds (37.5 kg). Yet I've never had a table collapse or

even groan under the weight of a garden I've placed on it and have kept on it for years.

The kind of table probably most commonly available for gardening is the disused patio table with a wooden top, perhaps weathered to the point of decay from years spent outdoors. Depending on the degree of weathering, on the thickness of the tabletop boards—ideally 1⅝ inches (4 cm), safely 1¼ or 1 inch (3 or 3.5 cm) thick, daringly ¾ inch (2 cm)—and on whether or not the boards have been treated with preservative, a garden on a wooden-topped table may be safe from gravity for as long as 20 years or as short a time as 3 or 4. Plan on gravity calling time on the table garden eventually, and while keeping that limitation casually in mind, enjoy the extraordinary mesa verde of your making. But check on the condition of the table's boards once a year using a trowel or a knife to dig a test hole down through the soil to the wood.

Wood preservative brushed on the tabletop before installing the garden may lengthen the life of the boards by years. For the health of the garden wait at least a few days after applying the preservative before you place soil and plants on the table, time enough for fresh air and rain or repeated hosing to dissipate much of the poison that remains unabsorbed on the surface of the wood. Even with the use of preservative, though, the boards will eventually rot. Before they give way, the table garden may be cut into sections with a chef's knife or a machete, taken off the table piece by piece as you would a lasagna from a pan, and set aside; count on a dense mesh-work of roots in the soil to keep each segment of the garden from crumbling. Replace the boards with new ones cut to fit, and reinstate the garden on the restored table, or transplant the garden onto a newer table. Even after years in place tabletop plants usually move safely, due to their compact root systems, but avoid cutting into soil close to the trunk or crown of any plant.

Beside tabletops made of wood, those made of various other materials can be equally suitable for table gardening and may be longer-lived. My own table gardens include compositions on a metal table (rusting steel, doubtfully as enduring as a good, thick wooden tabletop); a table with a

translucent plastic top (at least as long-lived as wood); tables topped with stone slabs of relative immortality; and several small tables made of "pressed wood"—an aspic of wood pulp and plastic—about which I will have more to say later.

I have yet to use a glass-topped table as a base for a garden that covers the *entire* top of the table, having never owned a table with thick enough glass. The usual quarter-inch (6-mm) thickness

PLATE 84. Autumn maples on a glass-top table.

PLATE 85. A *Medinilla* shrub and African violets grow on a hand-carved hardwood table in tropical highland. The *Medinilla*, collected in nearby mountain forest, is one of some two hundred species endemic to the Philippines.

might prove to be inadequate for a garden weighing even as little as 50 pounds (25 kg). Three-eighths-inch- (9-mm-) thick glass would probably be strong enough for a garden weighing about 100 pounds (50 kg), although I would still be leery of piling on stones. Meanwhile, without concern, my brother Ken, his wife, Phyllis, and I have on display, *at the center* of a glass tabletop a quarter-inch (6-mm) thick, a grove of dwarfed maples and of mosses (Plate 84) weighing about 35 pounds (17 kg). The display is left in place as an unobtrusive center piece during day-to-day use of the table (morning coffee or sundown drinks in the garden), but is lifted off and set aside in preparation for the occasional dinner party that will take up all the table surface.

What do you do if you are primed of mind to create a table garden but have no usable table of any kind? You might carpenter a table (Plate 85), or you might construct one of stones. If you have no wild-found stones for the job, look for some usable specimens in the sales yard of a dealer in stones for landscaping. Find a reasonably flat slab of granite or limestone or of some other geology that is about 20 to 40 inches (50 to 100 cm) in diameter to serve as a tabletop. Find as well, smaller stones of varying sizes to use for a table leg—when fitted or cemented together into a column. A columnar table leg of about half the diameter of the tabletop will be broad enough to support the top without its being overly tippy if you lean on one side of it. Or you might buy only

PLATE 86. Treelets on a table assembled from stones selected in the yard of a dealer in rocks for gardens.

the stone slab and mount it on a sawed off length of tree trunk tall enough and broad enough to make a table leg—if you should be so lucky as to have such raw material.

Plate 86 shows a table I've assembled from dry (uncemented) stones. Field stones form a central leg on which a flagstone top is balanced. The term "field stone," in its original usage, applied to stones found scattered in fields. In the argot of today's stone trade, field stones are also those exfoliated from mountain-side outcrops—and such are the stones that I've used; they were brought down from the Cascade Mountains. (The flagstone came from Arizona.) Rusty brown *Carex comans* and bluish-green *C. glauca* grow lustily on pavement near the table, in soil 4 inches (10 cm) deep, edged and retained with *Sedum album*. My sharp-eyed reader will spot the maple grove on *this* table as being the same one in another color plate—there growing years later, on another table, at a different season, in a different garden.

If table construction isn't for you, you might shop for one, as I've also done. I went looking for an appropriately small table for a small garden I envisioned. Where to find such a table, one that would serve my purpose and that I could bring myself to buy? Not, as it turned out, at used furniture stores, which I investigated all over town. I may have been singularly unlucky in my quest, but all I found were indoor tables of fussy styling that would have made them appear ridiculous as a platform for the naturalistic garden I had in mind.

At a display of new garden furniture on the pavement outside a supermarket, I paused over a good-looking, all wood patio table, bigger than I needed but very tempting at $200. But no, the price, which seemed reasonable to me, the appassionnato table gardener, was deemed outrageous by certain dour ancestors of mine, hardscrabble farmers in eighteenth-century colonial America, who get through to me at times on some genetic channel.

As a last resort I entered one of those warehouse-type emporiums, a place where scarce clerks hide away amidst cavernous aisles stacked toward the ceiling with hardware and household furnishings, including small tables that come flat in boxes. I decided on a little, round-topped, assemble-it-yourself number, priced at only $17.00. The table's plain styling suited it well enough to table gardening; however, the material from which it had been

PLATE 87. Woodlanders in the shade of a dogwood tree.

PLATE 88. Detail of the woodland table; *Begonia grandis* in flower; the fern *Athyrium nipponicum* 'Pictum' in silvery green leaf.

made, "pressed wood," lacked élan. The flat table sections had a doughy pallor and the mealy feel of a graham cracker, but two coats of brown deck paint converted the highly improbable into the plausibly gardenable. I went ahead with my table garden and have been satisfied enough with the results to have purchased additional tables of the same design. These irresistibly low-priced but chintzy little tables of ¾-inch- (2-cm-) thick "wood" last only about 3 years as garden platforms; two of them have already been replaced. But, to carry on with the gardens they have supported, all that we (two of us working together) have needed to do has been to lift the garden from the tabletop and onto a new table of the same kind. Three years of root growth, along with the natural conglomeration of soil that has been in place for a time, hold the garden together while it is being transplanted in toto. But any large stones are removed before the transplanting—leaving cavities (conglomeration at work) the exact shape of the buried portion of the stones. With these cavities as guides, the reinstatement of the stones is an easy matter, once the soil-and-plant part of the garden has been newly placed. If all this seems to you to be table gardening over the top, I admit to it.

What Kind of Plants?

What kinds, out of the countless available varieties of plants, might a person grow on a tabletop? Answer: Almost any. Almost any plants that are unquestionably hardy in your climate and not outsize for the table, or which can be maintained at a suitable size and shape by pruning, are suitable for a table garden. Treelets and shrublets or trees and shrubs kept pruned, garden perennials of middling and smaller sizes, cacti and other succulents, annuals, woodland flowers, ferns, epiphytes, aquatics (in a water-tight container nestled in the tabletop soil), mosses, and lichens are all good candidates. Except for aquatics, I've tested representatives of all these plant categories in my table gardens and all have stayed healthy and kept growing. But I must emphasize that plants tend to be a little less hardy in a table garden than when grown in the open ground. Avoid those kinds that winter uncertainly in your area, and base your gardening on plants of tried-and-true hardiness.

In Plate 87 a table in the shade of a dogwood tree is chockablock (not to say crowded—I like it this way) with ferns—*Polypodium vulgare* 'Cornubiense' (at left), *Athyrium nipponicum* 'Pictum' (at center)—and other hardy woodlanders, including *Begonia grandis* (at top). In the close-up view of this table (Plate 88), the *Begonia* displays its summer flowers and the *Athyrium* its silvery green elegance. It seems safe to say that a majority of the hundreds of kinds of woodland plants available from specialist nurseries and at garden centers will grow easily on a shady table. The only exceptions I can think of would be plants too tall or too bulky to accommodate.

Soil and Fertilizer

Commercial planter or potting soil mixes that contain sand or pumice in addition to humus are entirely suitable for table gardening. Such mixes are usually made up primarily of humus—rotted plant material such as tree bark or sawdust, sphagnum or sedge peat—with perhaps a 25-percent portion of builder's sand or a lesser amount of pumice blended in. They often contain a short-term supply of fertilizer as well. Some deluxe mixes contain helpings of actual soil (loam or topsoil) and even animal manure, in addition to the other ingredients I've named. Such blends are also to the taste of table garden plants. Whatever mix you buy, be sure to get one that has sand or pumice in it. These ingredients

PLATE 89. Beside a garden path in tropical highland a hand-carved table holds a little jungle of rain forest driftwood, ferns, terrestrial orchids, and flowering *Schlumbergera*. About the legs of the table grows the white-variegated *Ophiopogon jaburan* 'Vittalis'.

have great value in reducing the compacting and caking of the soil over time, to an eventual state of airlessness. All table garden plants except aquatics, in fact, all terrestrial plants wherever grown grow better with a plentiful supply of air in their soil. If you will be making up your own soil mix, a good, airy recipe consists of a blend of two parts humus (preferably sifted) to one part sand, and as optional ingredients, one part loam and a scattering of fertilizer.

Plants growing in a mix that contains long-lasting fertilizer usually need no additional feeding during the first several months after planting. After that time, feed the garden with an occasional helping of long-life fertilizer beads, or with a diluted liquid fertilizer applied about once a month during spring, summer, and fall.

Composing the Garden

If the table on which you will place soil has a board top with spaces between the boards, spread newspaper several sheets thick to cover the spaces, or cover them with maple, oak, or other large leaves. The covering will keep soil from falling through when you shovel it onto the table. By the time the paper or leaves rot, plant roots will hold the soil securely. Here let me repeat a vital point I've made earlier on: Work with soil that is dryish and crumbly enough to be poured from a shovel blade as if it were dry cereal poured from a box. Soil that is wet and cloddish, like stiff oatmeal or grits, should be left to dry before you use it. Shovel soil onto the table to a final depth, after compacting it by slapping it with a back of the shovel blade, of 6 to 9

inches (15 to 23 cm). To create a hilly or cliffy landscape, build the soil up to a compacted depth of about 9 inches (23 cm) at one or more places on the tabletop, and hold it in place with stones, driftwood, or a closely spaced planting of a ground cover.

Place soil to within about 1½ inches (4 cm) of the table edge. Slope this edgewise soil at a stable angle of 45 degrees, and protect it from erosion by planting it closely or stonewalling it. With the use of stones or other solid shoring, the soil near the table edge could be steep or even vertical and would still be secure.

Stones or driftwood (never the two together, please; they fight esthetically) are useful not only in shoring the soil but also in uniting the tabletop composition—drawing it together magnetically. A single stone or a piece of driftwood may provide sufficient magnetic power, and several stones or driftwood pieces may do the job even better—or may not, as your artistic self will decide.

In the making of a naturalistic garden, weathered stone conveys much more of Nature than does quarried rock. Where several stones are placed together in a garden, a unity of species—having them all of granite or sandstone or some other mineral—produces a more serene effect than a geological mishmash. Arrange stones (or driftwood) on the tabletop after placing the soil, yet before going ahead with the planting. Be prepared to shift the positions of anything and everything in the garden—plants, stones, or driftwood—to fit all together in a way that pleases you, the landscape gardener. Don't lose heart over not getting it right on the first attempt; that's entirely usual. Given that all artistry is drawn from the same well, consider your efforts to be of a piece with those painstaking adjustments a Rembrandt or a Raphael made in their works, as proven by the under-painting that shows up in x-ray photography or whatever the technical name for it.

Driftwood may be placed in a table garden so that it lies entirely within the rim of the table or, if the piece of wood is lengthy, it may be cantilevered far beyond the table edge, dramatically enlarging the tabletop garden, as seen in Plate 89. If you go looking for driftwood, not all of it is to be found by beachcombing. There is also inland driftwood, to be fossicked for in logged off areas and elsewhere, even in an alley where somebody may have tossed a handsome tree root or two.

By the time the table garden is 1 or 2 years old, the airy soil mix, the kind that is best for plant growth, will have naturally settled and lost some of its airiness and volume. Most settling occurs during the garden's first couple of years, lessening the soil's depth by about one-third, even after the compacting you gave it when constructing the garden. No harm to the plants as a rule. However, if the settling seems excessive, top-dress the garden with new soil to compensate for the reduction of the old. Most kinds of plants, including even shallowly rooted, easily smothered rhododendrons and other ericaceous species, will welcome a ½-inch- (13-mm-) deep top-dressing with an airy soil mix every 2 or 3 years. Those plants that may be harmed by top-dressing (such as cushion-forming cacti and ground-hugging mat plants) will not mind being bottom-dressed. This is done by lifting the garden from the tabletop (either entire or in cut-apart portions), shoveling a couple of inches of soil onto the table, and then replacing the garden—with little twisting and wriggling adjustments (the like of those a dog makes in nestling down comfortably) to settle roots into the blanket of new soil.

Watering

The water requirements of a table garden are the same as for thirsty pot plants or tub plants grown outdoors: daily watering, or near-daily watering, is in general the regimen. If you are good at keeping container plants watered, your experience demonstrates that you have the stick-to-itiveness to be a master at table garden maintenance. But even if the pot of petunias or the tubbed Japanese maple withers in your hands, you can still table garden with the many available kinds of drought-tolerant plants: These may yet make a ten-green-fingered prodigy of you.

Xerophytic plants aside, the table garden placed in sun and planted with sun-loving annual, perennial, or woody plants with average moisture requirements will need to be watered nearly every day during those spring, summer, and autumn days when no rain falls; *nearly* every day for reason that there will sometimes come a day or two or even three after a rain—days with lingering dampness and no wind—when the garden will retain moisture enough to need no additional water. But a table garden of shade-loving plants properly placed in shade or a garden of sun-lovers placed in half shade may not need daily watering even in sunny weather. Here is a simple test of the water needs of any table garden: If the soil surface is moist, or if the surface is dry but the soil is moist a quarter-inch

(6 mm) down when you scrape at it with an inquisitive finger, the garden should be able to get by without being watered until tomorrow. This is a spring, summer, and autumn test. Water requirements in winter are as needed to keep the soil slightly moist.

A table garden of drought-tolerant plants—cacti and dozens of other genera of succulents, among them *Sedum, Sempervivum, Crassula, Aeonium,* and *Echeveria,* or a garden of *Sansevieria*—will grow and flower the more spiritedly when watered deeply, if not daily, perhaps twice weekly or as infrequently as once every week or so during their growing season in the warmer months of the year. These plants are unexacting and will withstand weeks of summer dryness, or will gladly soak up a daily dousing, as long as the soil is porous and fast-draining, protecting them from root rot. By the way, drainage has always proved to be adequate in my own table gardens, even on those tables with solid tops impervious to water—which in that case drains entirely from the table edges.

In our Pacific Northwest gardening, my garden friends and I don't water our cacti at all during winter, or at least not until the transitional time of latest winter and earliest spring. The cacti are brought indoors in October and left unwatered until early February, when they are given one deep watering; they receive a second watering in late March or early April, and are taken back outside in May, well after any expected frost. In our tropical gardening, other garden friends and I leave our cacti out in the rain year-round (but *Mammillaria* and other woolly genera won't survive the rainy season).

In Plate 90 a rustic table with a top made of a solid slab of wood 2 feet (60 cm) in diameter supports a desert scene of cacti and other succulents amid stones. I've used a sandy, fast-draining soil built up 9 inches (23 cm) high on the tabletop, with steep soil edges retained by the stones and the plants. The composition is held together visually by the use of stones related in form and color—they are all the same geological species of silt-stone—and by a repetitive planting of five dwarf cacti: *Cereus peruvianus* 'Monstrosa'. These stand tallest of all on the table and suggest, to my eyes at least, a group of saguaro (*Carnegiea gigantea*) in a Sonoran Desert community. The dwarf *Cereus* is one of the easiest small cacti for outdoor cultivation in all summer rain and mugginess, when such days come, but is not hardy in a cold, rainy winter. This entire garden could, however, be taken indoors. Table, stones, soil, and plants weigh less than 200 pounds (100 kg), not too much for three people to carry into a greenhouse or conservatory for the winter. If it happens, though, that you are gardening in a desert or in a Mediterranean-type climate, a deserty table garden plant community such as this one will probably be weather-proof year-round.

The water requirements of any table garden are those of the thirstiest plants in the composition, usually making it impractical to combine drylanders and moisture lovers, unless you can with fair precision direct the hose or watering can to the plant that demands moisture, and away from the plant that really doesn't need it—as I do with my

PLATE 90. A grove of cacti and other plants amid boulders make up a desert scene.

occasional table garden combinations of incompatible drinkers. My own table gardens are located on home properties in several countries that I visit each year, but where I stay only several months at a time. When I'm in residence I myself water the table gardens (only one of the gardens receives water automatically, the rest manually). When I'm away my garden friends take care of the watering. For these friends I've demonstrated the finer points of table garden irrigation: the directing of a soft spray straight downward on all parts of the table garden surface, the care not to miss any of the garden's edges. But still I have lost—*we* have lost I should say, to include the erstwhile waterers—several shrubs that grew at the far sides of the gardens, table sides which in these instances were less easily reached with the hose. I've replaced the shrubs, repeated the lessons in watering, and have wondered at times that my enduring friends have never turned the hose on me.

A Garden Safe from Many Pests

The table garden, on its platform well above ground level, is usually fully protected from dogs, rabbits, and—if the table's legs are unclimbable by furry feet, and if there are no overarching tree branches—from rodents as well. The table garden is considerably protected from crawling insects such as weevils and caterpillars, and also from slugs and snails. On a table, I am able to grow small *Campanula* species that are caviar to the mollusks, plants that I've lost every time I've yielded to springtime impetuousness and planted them in the open ground. But a few insects and mollusks will

inevitably climb the table's legs to its top, or will have been installed as stowaways during the placing of soil and plants.

In my own table gardens these unwelcome guests will find lethal little helpings of toxin-laced apple pomace waiting beneath overhanging rocks or beneath cozy canopies of leaves. Poisoned pomace is, in my experience, the most effective and longest-lasting bait for snails and slugs; garden stores offer it under several brand names, but if you can't find it, other kinds of bait will also kill mollusks. Weevils, though, usually won't touch any kind of bait despite claims made by manufacturers. Only hand-picking at night, when weevils come out from their hiding places to feed, is effective. And not even the most seductive bait will draw every mollusk to its just deserts.

Other ways to achieve full protection from all nasty critters (except those that come on wings or were installed with the garden) include fixing a tanglefoot preparation to the table's legs or placing the table's feet in pots filled with oil, as I once saw being done in a Tokyo suburb to protect a backyard collection of vulnerable alpines in containers kept on tables. Not a pretty sight, those boots of oil, but they worked perfectly in keeping the goodies from snails in a surrounding plagued with their numbers.

Believers and Non-Believers

It remains for me to alert you to the probable social consequences of your taking over a table for this audacious and startling enterprise. Prepare yourself for encounters with believers and non-believers in your efforts. Table gardening has proved to be so unexpected to certain gardeners who have seen one or another opus tabularis of mine that the sight has provoked strong reactions ranging from delight to dismay. The latter has come from folks with repressed imaginations whose sense of the righteously customary use of tables has been offended. I can see it in their faces even if they don't say a word, as they usually don't. They glance at the table garden and walk on wordlessly.

Countering such dismissals are the responses of certain individuals in the garden club groups who have visited my friend Nancy D. Short's lakeside property, where I have one of my table gardens—ours I should say. Nancy tells me that the tabletop landscape of ferns, stones, and moss has elicited more interest from her visitors than has any other feature in her sizable garden, which I know to be a visual feast.

While I'm here at Nancy's place, I want to pass along an idea of hers and also of another of my garden friends, Mo of Auckland. Both of these women have worked with the physically handicapped, and it has occurred to both that table gardening could become a valuable activity for paraplegics. Tabletops are usually high enough that a wheel chair could be maneuvered in closely to allow a person's arms to reach all parts of a tabletop garden, right to the center. The table would of course have to be especially sturdy and stable, next to impossible to overturn if knocked against by a wheelchair.

What a sailingly good idea: this practical application for a kind of gardening that makes little other claim for practicality, but much for adventure.

CHAPTER EIGHT

Table Garden Tours

Examples of table gardens follow, beginning with
the one at Nancy's mentioned at the end
of the previous chapter.

Fern Table

On Sunday I had a group of six ladies who had bought a package tour of my garden and others to support the Chase Garden
[a great home garden in need of a future]. The tour was a birthday present from one of the tourists to her mother, whose 76th
birthday it was. Also included were four of her mother's
friends. And all were pop-eyed over the fern table, enjoyed having the plants up off the ground, found them easier to see and
admire.

—*From a letter written to me by NANCY D. SHORT*
four summers after my planting a table garden on her property.

PLATE 91. Table garden
mainly of ferns, pho-
tographed soon
after planting.

This is how the fern table came to be: For years, whenever I visited my garden friend Nancy, a magazine editor, I would walk by an elegantly plain oblong table of blackened steel legs and frame, with a top of cedar planks, that idled in an alcove beside a garden path leading to Nancy's front door. The table was never in use, always bare;

the alcove in which it stood had been retired as well, superseded by other garden areas where people gathered nowadays, newer green rooms created in the revising of an old garden. I visualized a livelier future for the abandoned table and finally asked Nancy to let me convert it into a "garden party of small-growing ferns," as I described the project. "Sounds interesting, let's do it!" she replied, keen as always for things new in the garden. It was to be my gift to honor her 85th birthday, though given

PLATE 92. Fern table 5 years after planting. The table-edge conifer at left is *Microbiota decussata* about 12 years old.

somewhat in advance of the day since I would be away at the time. I made an appointment for Nancy and myself with nurserywoman Judith I. Jones, a fern specialist whose catalog that year listed a variety of species whose sizes seemed right for the table garden.

On the morning of our trip to the nursery, I built some tall sandwiches, pastrami and chicken on olive bread, fortification for the day. It would be lunch time when Nancy and I reached the nursery, located in foothills of the Cascade Mountains, inland from our Seattle-area homes. Judith, a vegetarian, as I discovered, politely declined my sandwiches; our hostess nibbled some kind of wholesome fodder while we two carnivores tucked into our indefensible fare.

After lunch on the nursery grounds I picked up a stick and scratched, in the bare earth of a service area, a 3-by-9-foot (0.9-by-2.7-m) outline representing the dimensions of the oblong tabletop. Then I encouraged Nancy and Judith to select a variety of small-to-middling ferns, up to about a foot and a half (45 cm) tall, and assemble them within the outline I'd made on the ground, ferns enough for a full planting on a tabletop just that size.

I do believe that my two friends had a grand time making the selections. I wandered off, studying ferns on my own in the extensive nursery grounds, but kept close enough by to hear at least the lively tone of their conversation, and the cooing notes of a charmed gardener, meeting and greeting the more winsome of the ferns for the first time. Twenty-five ferns of ten kinds, whose names I'll supply later, filled the space I'd outlined. I had,

however, made a dumb mistake in the measurement, which actually turned out to be dumb luck.

The next day, while composing the fern table in Nancy's garden, it dawned on me that the table outline I had scratched in the ground accounted only for the surface measure of the tabletop and not the measure of the sidewise slope of the soil I would place on it. After shoveling and leveling soil on the table to an even depth of 7 inches (18 cm), and sloping its sides for stability, I found that the soil's slope measured 9 inches (23 cm) top to bottom by nearly 24 feet (7.3 m) long—a little less than the perimeter of the table, since I'd set the soil back an inch (2.5 cm) or so from the table edge to minimize spillage while I worked.

Good! There would be room for a grander tabletop landscape than I had at first visualized. There would be room for stones, always a source of instant gravitas and calm in a newly made garden, where small plants left to themselves tend to stand about in nervous and tentative posture. Happily, I had some stones on hand, glacier-shaped loaves of gray granite dating from the latest Ice Age, a fine textural and tonal complement to the green and lacy ferns.

The stones came first, a spare number arranged to suggest natural outcrops by partly burying them in the tabletop soil. Several additional stones set into the gravel beneath the table connected the tabletop composition with terra firma. Ferns came next, along with clumps of dwarf perennials (*Astilbe simplicifolia* and *Epimedium alpinum* in named forms), planted between the tabletop stones. Then came cascading plants placed along the edgewise slope of the soil, notably the Siberian

conifer, *Microbiota decussata*, wonderfully useful in table gardening as an edging plant. This shrub is more usually a cushion-forming ground cover, but when planted on its side with its branches leaning downwardly from the table's edge, the *Microbiota* will carry on growing in that direction year after year—not with the straight down plunge of a waterfall, more with the cascading turbulence of a steep mountain stream. As a finishing touch I placed an upholstering of moss on all the soil not covered by the ferns and other plants, a moss of the genus *Homalothecium* (Plate 91), flat-growing,

PLATE 93. The fern table with *Astilbe simplicifolia* 'Sprite' in bloom and with oak fern (*Gymnocarpium dryopteris*) in full fig and ready for mischief (a move in on its neighbors) near the table's left-hand edge. The plant hanging from the table edge at center is an outstandingly valuable club moss (a *Selaginella* or *Lycopodium* species) brought back from Japan without an identifying label.

sheet-forming, chartreuse-colored, collected by peeling it off a shaded shed roof.

In the 5 years that have gone by since the day of planting, the fern table at Nancy's has developed into one of the best cases for table gardening I can make (Plate 92). It gets better looking every year, there in its half-shaded alcove. Daily in summer the table garden receives a special tonic: Sprinklers deliver untreated water pumped up from Lake Washington a few hundred feet downhill, a clear but rich soup of dissolved humus and microorganisms. Maintenance of the garden has been an easy matter. After 3 years in place, the dwarf *Astilbe* and *Epimedium* had expanded their territories to the point of overgrowth. With a sharp knife I excised portions of the plants without lifting them entirely. With new soil to fill the excisions, and moss to cover, almost no sign of the surgery remained even immediately after it had been done. Occasional weeding is needed for as usual the world over, breezes and birds bring weeds as seed. Spent fern fronds are removed routinely in springtime; left in place over winter they comfort sleeping crowns.

Of the original ten kinds of ferns, a majority have grown splendidly. The successes are *Arachniodes simplicior, Asplenium scolopendrium, Athyrium nipponicum* 'Pictum', *Dryopteris dissentiana, D. sacrosancta, Polystichum tsus-simemense,* and *P. xiphophyllum*. A load of Latin, that. The ferns that have failed at table gardening include a couple of dwarf clonal selections of *P. setiferum* (better suited to an alpine house or cold frame, I would think), and a cliff fern native to the Sonoran Desert (ferns of desert origin are always winter-touchy when attempted outdoors in a maritime climate such as that of Seattle and vicinity).

Nancy on her own has added the oak fern (*Gymnocarpium dryopteris*) to the fern table (Plate 93), along with one other fern I would like to tell you about in a moment. Both species have truly

added to the garden composition. As for the oak fern, a roaming ground cover, I was concerned that it might be invasive, but table garden culture has restrained it just enough—up until now. Nancy's other addition is the tatting fern (*Athyrium filix-femina* 'Frizelliae'), with fronds 15 inches (37 cm) long but only an inch (2.5 cm) wide, the pinnae reduced to little rounded fans. This is certainly one of the planet's most endearing ferns. A Mrs. Frizell found it wild in Ireland in 1857, a single plant that "grew between two boulders so fast and with so little soil," so she recalled, "that it was with great difficulty that my husband removed it." What a find, one that we are lucky to have inherited. A century and a half later it carries on as heartily as ever.

Ferns. They bestow on their growers one of the greater gifts of plants to people. With their wingy and feathery forms ferns are, you see, uplifting.

Beach Scene

In seikei, the Japanese garden art of scaling down dramatic scenery to fit into tray-form containers more or less the size of scatter rugs, a favorite theme is the islanded plant community. Tiny but gnarly trees and often shrubs as well grow on rocky islands that arise from a waterway. The ensemble has about it an astonishing realism in miniature. I had an idea for a table garden distantly related to such seikei landscapes, but unlike them in being more abstract than realistic.

The garden would have a focal feature, a boat resting on a rounded expense of gray sand at the center of the tabletop. Not really a boat, actually a fragment of pine bark I had picked up while on a woodland walk a couple of years earlier on, this flake of outer bark, 7 inches (18 cm) long, had dried and curled in just such a way as to have formed a narrow hull, an upswung prow and stern, in all the general appearance of a Viking long boat or a Venetian gondola. I had made a planter of it, filling the hull with several tablespoons of soil and miniature *Mammillaria* along with other little

cacti, four kinds in all, which have thrived (Plate 94). Now I visualized the pine bark planter as a cargo-laden vessel drawn up on a sand beach in my table garden to be. Inland, behind the beach, shrubbery would grow on raised ground, suggesting a woodland safely above the surge of waves in stormy weather. (A sense of fantasy is the designer here. Let your imagination return to the powers of about age 5 or 10 if you would create a scenic garden of this or of any kind on a tabletop.) At the foreground edge of my littoral landscape, along the table's rim, would be a number of plants of some

PLATE 94. This pine bark planter, with its miniature cacti species, inspired the table garden shown in Plate 97.

sort of fine-leaved ground cover of refined habit, to hold the garden's sand and soil in place.

Now all the plants that would make up the garden were unknown to me—to be discovered, I hoped, while plant shopping. Success seemed likely, since the locale of my project and my shopping was the city of Auckland, a horticultural hotbed. Off to a favorite garden center, then, to find an especially neat ground cover, together with shrubbery that would fit the tabletop, befit the beach front theme, and coordinate as a garden. It would, I decided, be interesting (a matter of Kiwi loyalty, of learning-by-planting, and of get-with-it fashionableness) to use some New Zealand natives in the table garden. And New Zealand horticulture was all ready for me. During the years that I've been gardening in Auckland—since 1977, for several months each year—the nation's nursery industry has been eagerly searching out and marketing new varieties of native plant species, particularly dwarf forms and color breaks in foliages. Nurseries here have in recent decades introduced hundreds of such varieties, and I fully expect that New Zealand horticulture will in time match that of another island nation, Japan, in *its* discovery and connoisseurship of thousands of variations of native plants over a period of centuries. Being islanded seems to stimulate the parsing of the indigenous vegetation. Yet, New Zealand is both a parser and, following an inherited British passion, an importer of plants. Both methods gain variety where variety is limited.

At the garden center I selected half-gallon- (2-liter-) container-size specimens of native shrublets labeled *Sophora prostrata* and *Weinmannia* 'Kiwi Red' (the name of the parent species had been omitted from its label). These plants, though new to me, appeared to have the potential to become sizable in time, but I felt sure I could keep them at table garden size; their twiggy habit would lend itself to creative pruning, as if for bonsai.

While there in the sales yard I sold myself four plants, in quart- (1-liter-) size containers (there were none smaller), of a compact form of thyme that would work as the ground cover or coverlet I needed. The four were labeled simply *Thymus* 'Pinkie'. Again, the nomenclatural omission and the resulting blank-out. For those of us who really care about knowing the plant we buy—its native place in the world if a species or its parentage if a hybrid, the experiences of other gardeners with this newcomer to our gardens—the lack of a Latin name usually amounts to the dead end of knowledge, or an added difficulty in learning. All that nursery folk would need to do to oblige us would be to include the binomial in parenthesis on the plant label below the jazzy sales name. Ah, well, 'Pinkie' had very much the appearance of a species of thyme, *T. cimicinus,* which I had grown in the United States decades before. The habits and values of 'Pinkie' should be similar to those of that relatively slow-growing, densely leafy species, and these were qualities I could use in my planting.

Before heading for the cash register I tested the table garden capabilities of my plant selections by arranging them on a newspaper pattern, a double broadsheet that I had, at home, cut and rounded with scissors to the outline of the 20-inch- (50-cm-) wide tabletop that would form the base of the garden. Now, I removed the folded pattern from a coat pocket and spread it out on a path in the sales yard. I saw that the two New Zealand natives and the four thyme plants would fit together on the small table easily enough as they did on the newspaper, and that there was need of a third shrublet, something with bigger leaves than those of the other plants, leaves not too big, though, about the span of a soup-spoon bowl—to serve as a foil for the smaller foliages I'd chosen. I had just the thing

PLATE 95. The pine bark planter with other plants in a garden mockup.

at home, growing in the open ground: *Nandina domestica* 'Pygmaea', a compact, mound-forming shrublet with varying green and orangey red leaves, the latter color at its brightest when the plant is grown in hot sun. 'Pygmaea' is one of New Zealand's most popular front yard greeters and has only this unfortunate over-use as a demerit. Otherwise, the plant is close to perfect and has in fact received a horticultural Oscar, an Award of Garden Excellence bestowed by the Royal New Zealand Institute of Horticulture. One of the many sterling qualities of 'Pygmaea' is that it can be divided and transplanted directly into open ground. Try that with any of the taller forms of *Nandina* and they will likely die, as I know from wretched experience. But, having had rewarding results in dividing up and transplanting 'Pygmaea' in years past, I now went out, dug up and clipped off just the right-size portion of the plant for my table garden.

The next step was to arrange all the major players on the tabletop—the *Nandina* and the other shrublets, the thyme plants, and the make-believe boat—in a rough mockup of the garden composition, to determine how best to fit everything together (Plate 95).

Planting Time. I began by removing the plastic pots and bags from all the garden center plants. The *Sophora* and the *Weinmannia,* as is common with container-grown nursery plants, had each formed a solid mass of roots pressed against the container bottom and sides, leaving the interior part of the soil mixture in the container almost barren of the young roots that absorb the plant's vital supply of nutrients and moisture. At 8 inches (20 cm) high the root-and-soil mass of these two half-gallon- (2-liter-) size shrubs needed to be reduced, since a maximum 7-inch (18-cm) depth of soil was as much as the small table could hold without risking an avalanche. As a remedy, I tore open the bottom surface of the shrubs' meshed roots and shook out the lowermost portion of the loose soil. It came away easily with minor damage to the plants' root systems.

After arranging the three shrublets (including 'Pygmaea') in a semi-circle at the far edge of the table to form a background for a garden that would be viewed from the front, I poured and tamped soil around the three, and retained the steep soil at the table's edge with stones ranging in size from that of bagels to that of bread loaves (Plate 96). The stone retaining seemed stark so I wedged the ground cover (and stone cover) *Selaginella kraussiana* into seams between the stones at their outward side. I, if no one else, would be examining this posterior quarter of the garden from time to time. The location I had in mind for the table garden—in a recess at the edge of a bed of shrubbery where it would be seen only from the front—dictated its front-to-back layout. Such an arrangement would probably appear awkward if the garden were to be located where viewers would walk all around it. In that case, its taller plants would be better planted more toward the center of the composition.

The four plants of thyme, placed in a semi-circle at the foreground rim of the table, formed a bulwark for the soil in their vicinity and provided the garden a trim front edge of fine, dark green foliage. Planted horizontally, with their foliage partly draped over the table rim, the thymes' root-and-soil masses proved not overly high for the tabletop, negating any need to shake away excess soil. But I did need leeway to top-dress the old root-bound, container-conformed cylinders of soil that had come with the thyme plants, so I pressed down on the cylinders flattening them considerably.

PLATE 96. Thyme plants laid on their side retain soil at the front edge of the table; stones hold the soil at the back edge.

Over the old I spread fresh soil an inch (2.5 cm) deep, and over that a layer of coarse gray sand (white sand would have been garish in this garden) whose particles were sizable enough to keep it from being dashed away by rain. With the positioning of the cacti boat on the sand the garden came together, became a beach scene (Plate 97).

Afterword. At present, the bark boat has weathered 4 years without decaying, and its cacti grow on with slow but unstinting enthusiasm. Since a couple of the species are woolly, and woolly cacti hate the cold rain of winter, the boat of cacti is removed from the table in the autumn month of April and placed near other wintering succulents, on a stand under deep eaves at the north (sunward) side of the house; the boat is returned to the table in the warmth of spring. As a winter replacement for the table garden's focal feature I've tried several objects found in Nature. The most effective of these is a small, water-smoothed, greenish gray stone embedded with fragments of fossil sea shells.

I would like to leave you with several names of alternative kinds of shrubbery, probably more readily available and perhaps hardier than the ones I've used, in case you decide to create a table garden which, like mine, requires upright shrublets. These should work well: *Hebe lycopodioides, Hypericum buckleyi, Jasminum parkeri, Leiophyllum buxifolium,* and *Paxistima canbyi.* All are twiggy, small-leaved, 1½ feet (30–45 cm) tall if unpruned. The *Hypericum,* a woody wildflower native to eastern American

mountains, has the added distinction of being on the Endangered Species List. Vanishingly rare in Nature, it is safely at home in rock gardens and specialty nurseries.

Marigolds on Stage

Plate 98 shows French marigolds (*Tagetes patula*) in a fiercely cheery chorus of summer flowers. They make great mood medicine. A person has only to pause for a look at this tabletop display and the whole world seems brighter, a lift to the senses that works in any weather but perhaps best of all on a dull day. Still more remarkable to me is the fact that I, who have found daily delight in these marigolds, had never before liked them in the slightest, had left them entirely out of a gardening career that goes back more than half a century. I've always been one of those gardeners—there are I believe many of us—with a limited appetite for yellow and orange hues (marigold colors) in a garden. Marigolds en masse are to me too hot and eye-hurting, a floral mob the mind associates with searing midday sun in garden places without sheltering shade. My table garden planting of marigolds was, then, an exercise of a contrary curiosity: Could table gardening make a disliked flower likeable? It could in spades! Plant marigolds on a table and the illusory optics of table gardening turn a few dozen flowers into an opulent bouquet of yellow and orange which seems not too much but just right.

In preparation for the planting, I spread a 2-inch (5-cm) depth of soil over the tabletop. And then, ahead of the marigolds, came the placing of

PLATE 97. Completed "beach scene" (if you will go along); the table has been placed at the edge of a bed of rhododendrons.

edging plants, vegetation of a kind substantial enough to grip and hold back the soil at the table's edge. I used *Chrysanthemum parthenium* 'Aureum', a compact, chartreuse-leaved form of feverfew; the species was a staple in medieval medicine, as a febrifuge. The form 'Aureum' lives on in the gardening world as a Victorian antique, still employed in pattern plantings and marshaled lineups. The plant in itself remains fresh and appealing despite all cliché usage. At a garden center, I filled a cart with pot plants of 'Aureum', as leafy as bib lettuces when bought. Ten of them, laid horizontally (Plate

PLATE 98. Marigold table—more than the gardener has bargained for.

PLATE 99. Feverfew (*Chrysanthemum parthenium* 'Aureum') serves as edging for a table garden of marigolds. As with the thyme edging shown in Plate 96, the feverfew has been planted horizontally with its foliage extending over the table's edge.

99) around the rim of a table 20 inches (50 cm) in diameter, covered and concealed the hard line of the table edge and would provide frilly-leaved leavening for the heavy flower heads of marigolds. These esthetic values of the edging plant were in addition to its sturdy usefulness as leafy shoring.

Next, fifteen plants of French marigolds, of 4-inch (10-cm) pot size, joined the 'Aureum' and filled the tabletop. The first to be planted—just above the 'Aureum'—were placed so that their foliage and flowers faced outward at a low angle of about 35 degrees. I poured loose soil over their roots to cover. Marigolds planted higher up and more toward the center of the table were placed at a steeper angle, while those planted close to the center were placed upright; all these plants were settled in with additional soil tamped about their roots. Planting most of the marigolds at angles presented their leafiest and most floriferous prospects to the viewer *at once*, no waiting during about 2 weeks of summer for the plants to grow, fan out, and look at you eye to eye with their flowers. Soil merely 6 inches (15 cm) deep at its deepest center-most area on the table has proved to be enough to keep the plants growing enthusiastically throughout summer—with the added help of an application of dilute liquid fertilizer every several weeks.

In this close garden community, the edging plant, *Chrysanthemum parthenium* 'Aureum', has required weekly pruning to keep it from fluffing up and growing over the lowermost marigolds. I've used household scissors (which allow even more sensitive surgery then would the use of secateurs) on this soft-textured, readily cut plant. It's an easy job, creatively satisfying, and even aromatically rewarding. When snipped, 'Aureum' releases a curiously agreeable blended scent of celery leaf, marjoram, and horse.

Afterword. The marigold table is located in Auckland, New Zealand, and in the early autumn of its first year I as usual migrated, flying to the Pacific Northwest to tend other garden projects. My Auckland garden partner, Mo, wrote to me saying that the marigolds and the feverfew had remained attractive well into autumn, and that when finally the composition began to look tatty she had replaced the flowers with winter pansies and replaced the edging plant, which had got out of hand for want of pruning (Mo is not a pruner), with a vigorous, yellow-green ground cover maddeningly labeled *Sedum* 'Golden Mound', with no species designation. More about this plant in the table garden tour entitled Bronze, Silver, and Gold.

Mosaic of Mosses

Moss mats of nine species have been fitted together in Plate 100 as a soil covering around a pair of Hinoki cypresses (*Chamaecyparis obtusa* 'Tindall') and around several weathered fragments of conifer driftwood, placed here in simulation of the surfacing roots of mature trees—the dwarf Hinokis, about 60 years old, certainly qualify. We gathered some of the mosses, illicitly, I suppose, in shrubbery beds within a city park only a few minutes' walk from the garden. The rest we gathered while on the same walk, by peeling them off a low mortared stone wall that parallels a sidewalk. These were taken with a glad conscience, not once looking over our shoulders, since city workers or others are known to jet-blast the wall clean of its magnificent coat of mosses periodically to bring the ugly quarry stone back into view.

The Hinokis grow on a cedar plank table in an ample soil depth, but away from the trees the

PLATE 100. Table mosaic of mosses; dwarf Hinoki cypresses (*Chamaecyparis obtusa* 'Tindall') form a centerpiece.

mosses have been provided with a mere inch (2.5 cm) of soil, plenty for them. These tabletop mosses capture, as a sweep of mosses always does, an atmosphere of serenity imbibed by the mind as a blessing not far from that of dropping off into a refreshing doze.

Bronze, Silver, and Gold

On the tabletop in Plate 101, quite like long human hair glistening in the sun, is the henna-bronze mane of *Carex flagellifera*, one of New Zealand's several carexes of like color, but not like any coiffure I've yet seen—except on a tribal fright mask, come to think of it. This species of tussock is distinctive for its fountain form and for its fantastically elongated seed-bearing stems—to 6 feet (1.8 m) long, a trailing snare wherever the plant grows in wilderness (rural New Zealanders call this tussock "trip-me-up"). In a table garden the long stems hang suspended and harmless.

The other plant on the table—an effective erosion-preventer here on a low slope of soil—is sold in garden centers as *Sedum* 'Golden Mound'. It appears to be a *Sedum* well enough, but as to its rightful identity and dignity, I have no idea. I'd love to know the plant's true prenomen and to be able to tell you that title. I can't bring myself to carry on repeating the soda pop name that some huckster has given the *Sedum* and will hereafter refer to it as "it" or as "the plant." It makes a quick and easy ground cover and edging plant in the tropical and the subtropical gardens where I grow it. The moss-like mat of chartreuse foliage, eye-catching but soothing, has never flowered for me

in the tropics (which may be just as well, as I'll explain). Here in New Zealand's North Island Mediterranea, flowers appear when the plant feels the urge—not every summer, and maybe only when, in times of drought, it becomes concerned about its legacy: Then it explodes into a mass of yellow star flowers, an effort that weakens and thins the neat, leafy mat. Clip off the developing stems of flowers to help conserve the foliage, or

PLATE 101. The lionine mane of *Carex flagellifera* trails from table-top to ground in this ensemble.

renew the plant from offsets. A single branch planted in springtime in any reasonable soil has the capability to expand into a near-foot- (30-cm-) wide mat by autumn. Both the *Sedum* and the *Carex* enjoy sun or part shade.

The silvery companion at the base of the table is the splendid *Astelia chathamica* 'Silver Spear', a New Zealand native of the lily family, now an up-and-coming landscaper's plant in England and along the West Coast of the United States. It is one of the boldest evergreen perennials hardy enough to chance in zone 6 or 5; an easy plant in fast-draining soil, sun or half shade; and a garden brightener especially effective with *Acanthus mollis*. 'Silver Spear' seems not to flower; it has not done so in the two decades that I've grown it. Hence, no seeds and no means of propagation, in my gardening at least, other than by division, using main might and massy steel. This *Astelia* grows as a dense clump, eventually forming a few offsets which are born with adult-size leaves and are separate from the parental clump on a mere inch (2.5 cm) of rhizome nearly as tough as wood. To gain new plants I sledgehammer the sharpened blade of a spade down through the rhizomes (it takes about ten good whacks). The divisions come away with tall foliage, a bit of rhizome, and shockingly little root. More than once I've thought, Well, I've surely killed this one; it can't survive with all that leafage and practically no roots. Nevertheless, I've never lost any of these seemingly impossible divisions and now have about a dozen thriving clumps of 'Silver Spear' in garden stations that need just such announcement as this silvery giant provides.

Cypress Cathedral

Plate 102 shows a tabletop miniaturization of one of my all-time daydreams as a landscape gardener. The full-scale dream is to plant a grove of columnar evergreen trees in open ground and watch them grow tall. The trees when planted would be of varying heights, with the expectation that they would remain varied as they grew; that way, they would always associate as a family instead of as so many units of arboreal architecture. And yet, walking within that grove would be grandly architectural in feeling, with something of the spiritual frisson one experiences in entering the hallowed space beneath ancient columns or medieval spires. Time itself would sit down beneath those trees and prop its back against rough bark for a rest and an amiable converse with the visitor sufficiently at ease with trees and time.

In nearly six full decades of gardening I've never yet had access to an expanse of ground and of sky suited to such a grove—there is the amicability of sky-sharing neighbors to be considered before planting a group of trees that would soon enough grow to be sky-filling. I've not given up on the idea full-size, but for now I have this tabletop planting of five yellow-needled Italian cypresses (*Cupressus sempervirens* 'Swane's Golden'). And I have found that much of what I've always expected to find in a major grove of trees is at home here in this minor one. It is only a matter of miniaturizing the daydream to go with the trees.

The cypresses were varied in height when planted, and as anticipated the grove has retained a familial relationship, the trees maintaining their

relative differences in height as they've grown. All's well, but all has not been perfect. In growing, a couple of the trees have tended to lean, and I have straightened them by plunging slim bamboo sticks into the soil close to their trunks in inconspicuous locations, and tying the sticks to the trees.

Italian cypress in any form is only half-hardy. Other spire-form conifers, fully hardy and equally usable in a table garden, include *Juniperus communis* 'Hibernica', *J. scopulorum* 'Blue Arrow', and *J. scopulorum* 'Blue Heaven'.

Summer Flowers, Winter Boughs and Berries

Each summer for several years I've filled a table in our Finn Hill garden near Seattle with colorful annuals and perennials. The latest summer display (Plate 103) combines the cascading *Lobelia erinus* 'Sapphire' with petunias, *Fuchsia magellanica* 'Tom Thumb', and *Artemisia absinthium* 'Lambrook Silver'. In autumn the table will be cleared, the annuals composted, the perennials planted in open ground (their root systems, compacted by table garden life, suit these plants to reuse easily on the summer table year after year). Then for the winter, the table is dressed up with a bouquet of cones, conifer boughs, and berry-bearing branches. It makes a good memory, the stroll through the garden on a crisp sunny day in late autumn, selecting things, as I have done for this winter's table display (Plate 104): boughs of spruce (*Picea engelmannii*), branches of *Pernettya mucronata* in

PLATE 102. Tabletop cypress grove; torch lilies (*Kniphofia*) in the open ground at back; a cabbage palm (*Cordyline australis*) beyond.

PLATE 103. A summer-winter table set with flowers. Photo by Ken Hollingsworth.

berry (I usually cut holly branches but the berries were sparse this year due to a lack of bees when the holly was in flower), and as a centerpiece a cockscomb of *Yucca glauca* foliage with an attached length of trunk that I've plunged into the tabletop soil (along with the branch ends of everything else). When the bouquet looks presentable, after considerable jiggering of the branches to fit them all together, I water it thoroughly, making sure the soil gets plenty. The bouquet stays fresh for months, well after the holiday season, whose celebrations I have foremost in mind when making the display.

About that *Yucca*: It is the same one I've been loath to de-barb, as discussed in chapter five, On Rocks and Railings. I have no hesitation, though, about sawing off whole trunks of the plant where they loll over our driveway, waiting to scratch cars.

Vireyas with Sculpture

The sculpture came long before the table garden in Plate 105. I'd had it on hand for 20 years in one place and another on our property before deciding to place it on a table surrounded by a complimentary planting. The sculpture, if indeed you will accept it as such, consists of the topmost 17 inches (43 cm) of an early twentieth-century wharf piling—hand-hewn Kauri wood capped with wrought iron—which I obtained in the nick of time from a workman with a chain saw. He was one of a crew dismantling a decaying wharf. The assemblage of wood and iron that he generously handed to me, in response to my asking if he could spare it, ranks as "found sculpture," a utilitarian object recognized as bearing resonances as well as being mundane. In form, it is an interplay of intriguing angles. It bears the marks of handwork and of age. It is a talisman of a regional history. In character it is mysterious and remains so even when you know the purpose for which it had been made and used. Quite a piece of art, an object with such emanative qualities.

I placed it on a table in a half-sunny location here in our garden on North Island, New Zealand (climate, Californian). Now to find plants that would work sympathetically with this particular piece of art and history. A surround of annual flowers? Ferns? Coleus? Mentally, I pictured each kind in turn around the sculpture, and each candidate appeared entirely possible, quite

PLATE 105. Vireya rhododendrons around a "found sculpture."

good-looking in the setting. But then I got to thinking that we—my Auckland garden partner and I—would probably find more return in an entire little landscape planted around the sculpture, a table garden featuring shrubbery of some kind. Mo, my partner, had lately become partial to Vireya rhododendrons, enjoying them for their surprise sessions of flowering from time to time

PLATE 104. The summer-winter table of Plate 103 in winter with boughs and berries for the holiday season.

throughout the year. All right, I would make a garden featuring Vireya hybrids (the species are mostly unobtainable) of compact nature, not dwarfs but slow-growers, slim and twiggy, easily controllable by pruning; Vireyas in a salmon-orange-vermilion range of flower color. These hot colors, which Mo and I enjoy in small amounts, would be accompanied by the harmoniously colored flowers of *Cuphea ignea* and by reddish-leaved forms of *Neoregelia* bromeliads.

Brought together on a table with the object d'art, the Vireyas and the other plants are not exactly a color harmony, but I'm not minding their minor jarring one against the other. Nature has far ruder clashes in the colors of single species of reef fishes, of rain forest insects, of parrots. If evolution sponsors cacophonies of color, a little gentle dissonance on my part ain't so bad.

None of the plants I've used will endure more than a couple degrees of frost, which we receive occasionally in Auckland. In a colder climate, as for example that of my Pacific Northwest garden, where winter brings, every few years, temperatures down nearly to 0°F (−18°C), I might have chosen for table gardening such hardy dwarfs among rhododendrons as *Rhododendron radicans, R. lepidotum, R. elaeagnoides,* and any of probably one hundred others. And to go with those shrublet rhododendrons, any of selected hundreds—surely—of the thousands of available alpine garden plants. *Saxifraga umbrosa* 'Primuloides', *Primula juliae, Linnaea borealis,* and *Geranium dalmaticum* come immediately to mind, but these are choices with no more preeminence than that of so many others.

Afterword. Mo, in a letter, tells me that she has especially enjoyed the Vireya table for its flowers and for its companionship. The table is part of the landscaping of a hideaway niche formed by a combination of table gardens, pavement plantings, off-the-pavement shrubbery, and teak-wood chairs, at a corner of our concrete parking area. The spot is now devoted to the ease of people rather than vehicles. Plate 25 shows this retreat, with the Vireya table partially in view at left.

Sansevierias and Seemannia

The plants in Plate 106 grow on a table topped with a natural slab of granite, and with a chain saw–sculpted cross section of log for legs. In flower is *Seemannia latifolia,* a Bolivian perennial of excellent garden value—winter-flowering for a couple of months, easy to grow in sun, and permanent. The small plants at the front of the table are the well-known *Sansevieria trifasciata* 'Hahnii'. The taller blade leaves belong to plain *S. trifasciata,* the major form of the species. This plant and its equally tall variety *S. trifasciata* 'Laurentii', the common mother-in-law's tongue with yellow-edged green leaves, are the toughest container/platform garden plants known to man—known to this man anyway. In my gardening experience, their nearest rival in tolerating seemingly impossible dimness of light, dryness, and foreverness in the same pot is the Norfolk Island pine (*Araucaria heterophylla*), but

PLATE 106. *Sansevieria* and *Seemannia* (in flower) on a granite slab, over a sculpted hardwood base.

mother-in-law's tongue takes the prize. Nearby the stone-topped table, I have 'Laurentii' growing happily under a foot bridge, a place dark enough to make a cat's eyes fire up in a flashlight beam. And in our home in New Zealand is a plant of *S. trifasciata* (not mine) that has been growing since 1977 in a 10-inch- (25-cm-) wide, 10-inch-deep glazed pot, with never a change of soil or a repotting. It is of help to the plant that the house, in common with most dwellings on New Zealand's North Island, has no central heating. The *Sansevieria* in the pot has not been watered for the past 6 months, as I know because I've been here, and nobody remembers when it was last fertilized. The leaf blades stand 3 feet (90 cm) tall, as is usual for the plant, which remains perfectly healthy. There may be a world record in this.

Faux Dwarf Conifers

The conifers in Plate 107 were as cute as kittens when I bought them at a garden center 2 years earlier and have not outgrown their cunning petiteness—as they surely would if I let them, which I won't. Nothing on their nursery labels indicated that they were other than plants that would stay dwarf. If I had not been acquainted with these very conifers from gardening experience and observation I might have gone home with them happily misapprehending their true nature. Dwarfs they are not. They belong to a

category of cultivated conifer varieties often supposed to be dwarf, sold and accepted as such, but which might be termed more realistically as intermediate growers. Rather than being truly dwarf they are only relatively slow growing at 4, 5, or 6 inches (10, 13, or 15 cm) or more yearly. In an astonishingly short time (as it must seem to a million gardeners in retrospection) such conifers will grow to be whoppers, exceeding their space if, as usual, they have been planted where there was need for them to stay small.

The number of intermediate conifer varieties in collections, in nurseries, and in garden centers totals many hundreds, with new forms being named and introduced year by year. Truly dwarf conifers certainly exist as well and are in the trade but number merely in the dozens. These are plants of extremely slow growth, an inch or two or three (2.5 or 5 or 7.5 cm) a year. At that rate, the conifer remains reliably small for decades.

I might have chosen such conifers for my table garden but did not, partly because they weren't available at the garden centers and nurseries I haunt. I might have searched for them in the mail-order catalogs of the few specialists in dwarf conifers but did not bother because I doubted extremely that these nurseries would have plants for sale at a size large enough to make much of an immediate showing on the table, preferably one-gallon (4 liter) container size. The prospect of waiting years for slow little conifers to grow to fill the stage sufficiently, making a garden of it, would seem to me too futuristic. I've reached an age at which my gardening future seems pretty much now.

PLATE 107. If they were in open soil the four little conifers on the table would grow like three hogs and a giraffe. Table gardening will keep them from getting out of hand.

So, my conifer table garden is made up of false dwarfs that I fully expect to keep small. The spare amount of soil on the tabletop will see to much of the dwarfing; pruning will accomplish the rest. The plants' limited root run, with its consequent restriction of root growth, results in restriction of above ground growth as well, but not as much as at the root. The color plate of the garden shows conifers that have grown with satisfying slowness, as expected. Pruning has amounted so far to a few minor snips; nor do I expect explosive growth in years to come.

The tallest of the four conifers on the table, *Juniperus chinensis* 'Torulosa', stands 26 inches (66 cm) and has recently been pruned back 4 inches (10 cm) at its summit—1 year's growth. If grown in the open ground this variety would attain a height of 15 feet (4.6 m) at about a foot (30 cm) a year. Second in size on the table is *Platycladus* (*Thuja*) *orientalis* 'Green Cone', 18 inches (46 cm) tall, eventually a 6-footer (1.8 m) when grown without restriction. *Chamaecyparis obtusa* 'Nana Aurea' is the third-tallest conifer here and would balloon upward to 4 feet (1.2 m) if unchecked. The table's fourth conifer, *Thuja occidentalis* 'Filiformis', whose varietal name describes its thread-form branchlets, has the will but not the means in this garden to grow 7 feet (2.1 m) wide and 5 feet (1.5 m) tall. In fact, I first knew this conifer as a specimen of about that size. It grew in a rockery beside our front steps when I was a lad in the 1930s and a teen in the 1940s, and it was my self-assigned chore each year to keep it cut back (sparingly, not butchering the plant) from our right-of-way. This was my first lesson in never underestimating the potential size and relentless determination to achieve it, which are in the spirit of the faux dwarf conifer.

Succulents as Seers' Plants

Plate 108 shows fifteen different kinds of plants with water-tank leaves growing happily together, if a bit dense by now. I foresee that with another year's growth, some thinning of their rosettes will be needed. The botanical trove includes, among other plants, echeverias, most prominently *Echeveria imbricata* with its big, open rosettes of glaucous leaves; various crassulas, among them *Crassula tetragona,* uppermost in the garden; and the somewhat exasperating *Pachyphytum kimnachii,* whose paddle-shaped leaves will at times, if you so much as touch them, detach, fall away, and seek places to root and grow into new plants. In Nature, kimnachii's leaves are probably knocked off by hard rain, the plant by evolutionary plan cannily taking advantage of the season of moistened soil to propagate itself vegetatively, but I'm only surmising as much. In garden conditions this propagation process may be helped along by gathering any fallen leaves, sticking them stem end down in a pot of sand, and keeping them slightly moist while they root.

Succulents prefer a steady supply of moisture while they are growing and require a soil porous and fast-draining. Their natural time of growth in their native lands is during the rainy season, at whatever time of year it comes, but in temperate zone gardens anywhere, these plants tend to grow

PLATE 108. Table full of succulents.

during the warmer months and to go dormant during the cooler part of the year. To keep them from stopping growth and going dormant in summer, keep them watered. I give my tableful of succulents a thorough watering twice weekly during summer and early autumn (no water during winter or in rainy springtime weather). Yet, these plants would easily survive weeks of summer drought in a state of dormancy if they were left on their own by gardeners away on vacation.

But more significant, I believe, than any tip I might give about the needs and ways of succulents, is an introduction to the pure pleasure they can bring to the visual gardener in most of us, the one who enjoys standing or sitting still while perusing plants, feeling for the moment no sense of duty toward them or anything else, simply experiencing the mental phase that I have heard certain others summon with the vibratory mantra "Om." When we reach this halcyon state of mind, each succulent plant we see invokes a distinct pleasure and tends to change in mind's eye into something other than itself, yet metaphorically alike. I stand beside this table of succulents and gaze at plant forms that easily transmute into jewelry, into brooches and medallions; into crystals; then into the plant-like animals of tidal pools.

What a shortcoming, it would seem, to be incapable of at least a little such mental wandering (a safe journey if brief) in the company of succulent plants. I discover, though, that not everyone is of the same mind. I'm thinking of the man who comes around to mow the lawn and other lawns in our neighborhood. Nice fellow. One afternoon as I stood removing spent leaves from this table garden of succulents, and grooming other table gardens nearby, at the edge of our parking area, he drove in, parked his panel truck, and walked over for a closer hello. He looked on as I puttered, glanced about for a moment, and then said that the trouble with my kind of gardening was that it took him too long to see everything—slowed him down too much. He said this in all seriousness, and I was astonished to hear it. I replied that being slowed down was the entire idea behind gardening as I see it: to have the garden provide entertaining detail that draws a person aside from any daily rush, to pause, look and relax. But I could see in his expression that he was not having it. We who garden visually will always remain a special breed of seers.

Tabletop Rock Garden

Supple knee joints, a thing of the past for some of us, provide the usual means of getting down near enough to meet and tend to small plants in garden beds. Table gardening offers a blessed alternative in bringing these plants up to a more humane zone of comfortable address. Another important advantage in growing the horticultural small fry on a table is that, in being more closely in view, they are apt to receive more attentive care, more weeding, watering, fertilizing, and grooming than is usually given to little plants growing in the open ground. While none of these advantages is any the less for plants *in pots* on a table, gardening directly on the table does away with the pots. There is no buying of

PLATE 109. This buoyant rock garden is a telling example of the floating quality of table gardening.

containers, no worry about over-wintering plants in crockery that might break during frost, no emptying and storing of pots through the winter, no wondering about where to put de-potted plants.

Miniatures suitable for table gardening are practically limitless. Of the thousands of species of rock garden plants now available from specialist nurseries and in rock garden society seed exchanges, almost any that are unquestionably hardy in your climate and are reliable in open ground–open sky cultivation year-round (quite a few are not) will do just fine in a table garden.

The community of miniatures brought together on the 30-square-foot (2.7-sq-m) tabletop partly in view in Plate 109 contains forty-four species of relatively easy-to-grow rock garden plants for a sunny location. Altogether, they make up a tight little island of greenery and flowers. I've kept the

more vigorous kinds edged back to prevent them from overwhelming slower growers. Surmounting all else in the garden is the treelet *Juniperus* × *media* 'Shimpaku'. *Veronica pectinata* spills from the table edge; behind it are mat-forming sedums, cushions of *Armeria caespitosa* (with pink pom-pom flowers) and, along with the many another minikin, a matlet of *Antennaria dioica* 'Nyewoods Variety' in rosy flower. For the latter plant, I claim a certain responsibility, having imported it from England in 1956. I'd become smitten by it while on a visit to Stuart Boothman's nursery in Maidenhead earlier that year. Some time later, I offered the *Antennaria* in my own mail-order nursery catalog, and so got it started in gardens in the United States. Garden plants seem to me a kind of benign social disease. They get around affectionately.

Index